Christamaria Fiedler

Pumpkin Crime

Aus dem Deutschen
von Sally-Ann Spencer

Thienemann

– 1 –

The mansion was huge – big enough to get lost in – and everything about it was **impeccably** stylish. It was Amanda's first visit, and she looked around with starry eyes. She didn't know much about the legendary Dr Black, but his mansion was divine!

"Isn't it fabulous?" whispered Isy. The two friends hurried down the long white marble corridor that connected the mansion's many rooms. "So, take your pick: do you want the conservatory, the dining room, the billiard room or the lounge? Or how about the ballroom, the study or the library?"

"I'll take the lounge," declared Amanda, squealing with delight at the pastel pink furniture. Isy opted for her favourite room: the library. The third member of their party, Isy's brother Benedikt, **lingered** in the corridor, then slipped into the study, which was connected to the kitchen by an underground passage.

Crucially for the investigation, none of them

---

mansion – herrschaftliches Wohnhaus;
impeccable – tadellos;
to linger – verweilen

were in the same room when the body was found. Predictably, the murderer refused to identify himself, so the three friends accused each other of the crime.

Amanda insisted that it must have been Benedikt, but he produced evidence to the contrary and pointed the finger at his sister instead. His accusation proved unfounded, but Isy was hot on the murderer's heels.

Slowly, she tucked a lock of brown hair behind her ear, and calmly accused her best friend Amanda Bornstein, otherwise known as Mrs Peacock, of killing Dr Black in the ballroom with a candlestick.

"How dare you accuse me?" Amanda said indignantly. "I was in the lounge all the time!"

From Amanda's reaction, anyone would think that someone had actually died. In fact, they were playing the popular detective game known as Cluedo. The board, divided into different rooms to represent an English country mansion, was famous throughout the world.

"I'll prove it to you," Isy told her, seizing the black envelope from the middle of the board and taking out the secret cards. She laid them face-up on the kitchen table and looked triumphantly at the others.

The first was a picture of the suspect, Mrs Peacock; the second was a picture of the room, namely the ballroom; and the third showed the murder weapon – a silver **candlestick**.

---

candlestick – Kerzenständer

Amanda stared at her blue plastic figurine. She was sure that Mrs Peacock hadn't done anything wrong. The murder could easily have been committed by Reverend Green, **aka** Benedikt, or by Isy's alter ego, Miss Scarlet.

Isy could tell from Amanda's expression that she still believed in her character's innocence.

"Listen, Amanda, the identity of the murderer was decided before we started playing. We put three cards in the black envelope – a suspect, a murder weapon and a room. You were destined to commit the murder. You didn't have a choice."

"So you're saying I should have suspected myself?"

"Exactly," said Isy. Benedikt, who had his sister's dark eyes and dark hair, smiled at Amanda encouragingly. "Don't worry, next time it might be me!"

"Next time?" Amanda stood up quickly. "There won't be a next time," she said decisively. "I don't like detective games. Trivial Pursuit and computer games are a million times more fun."

"Just one more round," pleaded Isy. "You'll see how good it is once you know the rules. It's all a matter of logic."

But Amanda had made up her mind. Grabbing her red jacket, she hurried out of the room, nearly stepping on Selma's **litter tray** in her haste to get away.

"Hey, hang on a minute!" shouted Isy, wondering why her friend was behaving so strangely. She

---

aka = also known as – alias; litter tray – Katzenklo

ran down the stairs and caught up with her just as she reached the front door.

"What's the matter? Are you angry because you lost?"

"Of course not! I'm in a hurry, that's all." Amanda pointed outside. The rain was coming down in sheets. "You'd better stay here. It's raining cats and dogs."

"It wouldn't be the first time I've walked you home in the rain."

"Who said I was going home?" Amanda pulled her hood over her long blonde hair and zipped her jacket all the way to her chin. "See you tomorrow! Bye!"

She galloped off like a wild pony, leaving Isy to stare after her in bewilderment. She wondered why Amanda wasn't going home. What on earth could she be doing at this time of night? And why didn't she want her to come with her? Isy and Amanda went *everywhere* together. She watched her friend disappear into the darkness, and suddenly she felt worried – and a bit suspicious too. Maybe Amanda was up to something. Maybe she had a secret that she hadn't told Isy.

Every fibre of Isy's body was tingling with **anticipation**. Without thinking, she set off after Amanda. She was halfway down the street before she realized that she was **snooping on** her friend.

Cars sped past, throwing up shimmering

---

anticipation – Vorgefühl;
to snoop on s.o. – jmdm. nachspionieren

droplets of spray. The cold water splashed into her face. A fierce autumn wind swept through her brown hair, but she walked on determinedly. She pushed her way through the crowds of people, hoping to catch a glimpse of Amanda's red jacket. Her friend had been behaving oddly for a while. Last Wednesday she had done a disappearing act as well. One moment they had been doing their homework together as usual; the next Amanda couldn't wait to make her escape.

Isy remembered what had happened the Wednesday before that. She and Amanda had been to the movies with Sassi and Bini, and Amanda had left without saying goodbye. At the time, she had blamed it on the crowds, but Isy didn't believe it. Three Wednesdays in a row was surely no coincidence. Something funny was going on.

According to Isy's calculations, Amanda had been acting strangely since the end of the summer holidays. She scanned the crowds impatiently, hoping to spot her friend. She couldn't think where Amanda could have gone. A person couldn't simply vanish into thin air!

Isy hurried on and eventually caught sight of Amanda. She was standing at a crossing beside a couple of sopping wet Bernese mountain dogs. They were waiting for the lights to change.

Mystified, Isy wondered where her friend was going. At that moment, the traffic stopped and Amanda crossed into a shadowy side street. A few metres later, she disappeared into a dark building. So that was it …

Isy looked up at the building and wondered what to do. The outside walls were old and **crumbly**, and the whole street looked **dingy** and grey. It seemed an unlikely sort of place for Amanda to visit. Maybe she knew someone who lived there. Isy couldn't think of any other reason why Amanda would visit the building. And she couldn't understand why her friend didn't want her to know.

Isy walked up and down on the spot, trying to keep warm. There were other strange things about Amanda's behaviour. It seemed to her that Amanda had changed. She was certainly more careful with her money. Amanda had stopped treating herself to hotdogs on the way home from school, and it was ages since they last went to Signore Georgio's amazing restaurant which served the best ice cream this side of Rome. She had even stopped buying treats from the bakery before school. The evidence was **irrefutable**: Amanda had stopped buying snacks. Isy had assumed that she was trying to lose weight, but now she wondered whether Amanda was saving the money for something else. What if Amanda was in trouble? Shivering with cold, Isy stared at the door of the building. The fact was, Amanda was keeping secrets from her, and it wasn't right. They were best friends, and best friends were supposed to stick by each other, no matter what. Amanda would have to be hiding

---

crumbly – mit abblätterndem Putz;
dingy – verkommen;
irrefutable – nicht zu verleugnen

something really important to break that rule. Surely she hadn't fallen in love? What if she had a secret boyfriend?

Isy had a sudden urge to burst through the door and find out what was going on. She thought about what Amanda would say if she suddenly walked in.

Shoving her frozen fingers deeper into her pockets, she decided to go home, warm herself up with a cup of tea, and talk Benedikt into playing another game of Cluedo. She would confront Amanda at school the next day. In her mind, she could see herself telling her friend that she knew she was keeping secrets, and she could imagine exactly how Amanda would react.

She would glare at her accusingly with her big blue eyes and **screech**, "Have you been spying on me, Isolde?"

— 2 —

Amanda glared at Isy accusingly with her big blue eyes and screeched, "Have you been spying on me, Isolde?"

The next lesson was sport. The other girls had changed into their games kit and were on their way to the gym. At the sound of Amanda's voice, they stopped and stared at the two best friends.

"I'm worried about you," said Isy defensively.

---

to screech – kreischen

"Every Wednesday evening you suddenly disappear. Something's wrong."

"Oh really? At least I don't spy on my friends!"

"Calm down, Amanda. I'm only trying to help."

"To help?" Amanda struggled into her pink **leotard**. "You're not trying to help. You're hoping that I'm up to something. You want me to be linked to some sort of crime that you can solve."

"Crime? I don't see how going on a *date* would be a crime!"

Amanda seemed **taken aback**. "And what's the name of my secret boyfriend?"

"How should I know? The Holy Ghost, perhaps?"

Silence descended on the changing rooms. Isy could hear the sports teacher shouting at their chattering classmates, who were supposed to be warming up. It seemed reasonable to assume that Amanda didn't have a boyfriend.

"OK, you weren't on a date. But there's definitely something wrong with you. I can see it in your face," she said, fishing for information.

Amanda stopped adjusting her pink headband and peered into the mirror. "What's wrong with my face?" she asked in alarm.

Isy stood behind her and looked into the mirror too. "Nothing, but you look kind of … worried. If something's bothering you, you should tell me, you know."

---

leotard – Gymnastikbody;
to be taken aback – verblüfft sein

"But you always make such a big deal out of everything."

"And you don't?"

"Yeah, but you're not the one who might be sent to prison." Amanda's eyes welled with tears.

"Prison? What are you talking about?" whispered Isy, **aghast**.

She was interrupted by a shrill blast on a whistle. The sports teacher was ordering the girls to line up.

"Amanda, you've got to tell me what's wrong!"

"I don't *have* to do anything!" Amanda glared at Isy defiantly and took a step towards the door. Isy blocked her way.

"Out with it, Amanda!" she demanded. "Imagine it was the other way round. What if I were in trouble and you wanted to help me. Wouldn't you want to know what was wrong?"

Before Amanda could reply, the door to the changing room flew open and Jennifer Niemann walked in.

"Everyone's waiting. The teacher wants to know if you need a written invitation?"

"Clear off!" hissed Isy, but Amanda seized her chance and rushed through the door.

But Isy's efforts were eventually rewarded. Later that day, towards the end of the sixth and final period, a ball of paper whizzed through the air and landed on her desk. It was a note from Amanda:

---

aghast – entsetzt

"OK, you win. We'll talk at Georgio's later. Amanda."

Georgio's was the Bornsteins' favourite restaurant, and Isy never failed to be impressed by Amanda's **unruffled** confidence. Without her friend, she would never have dared to enter such an elegant establishment. A **sheen** of sophistication covered the dark wooden floor, starched white tablecloths and cut-glass decanters, and the exotic aroma of fresh cappuccino filled the air.

Isy loved Georgio's, but on this occasion she was struggling to focus her full attention on Signore Georgio's delectable strawberry ice cream. She was dying of suspense.

"Go on then, Mandi," she said breathlessly. "Why would you be sent to prison?"

"Because I'm about to become a **forger**," whispered Amanda with a shudder. She popped a fresh strawberry into her mouth. "Forgers always get sent to prison."

"Not at thirteen years old!"

"OK, juvenile detention, then. It's hardly **a barrel of laughs**," said Amanda, dipping her spoon into a spiral of fluffy cream. She looked at her friend reproachfully; Isy didn't seem to understand the seriousness of the crime.

---

unruffled – gelassen, ruhig;
sheen – Schimmer;
forger – Fälscher;
a barrel of laughs – ein Paradies

The other diners were talking in hushed voices, watched over by Signore Georgio. He waved to Isy and Amanda from the counter. "How does it taste, *ragazze?"*

"Molto bene!" Amanda said weakly.

"Grazie!" said Signore Georgio, smiling. He balanced two glasses of grappa on a tray and served them to a nearby table where two ladies were discussing their problems. They were talking just loud enough for Isy and Amanda to hear.

"I haven't been on holiday for ages," one of them was saying. "I mean, I can't leave Hansi on his own. The neighbours used to look after him, but now they spend most of their time at their holiday home in Alicante."

"Tell me about it," sighed her friend. "I haven't been on holiday since the conservatory was built. A week or two at the seaside would be heavenly, but I can't afford to pay anyone to look after my plants. Students charge an awful lot these days."

"You and I need a couple of angels to help us out!"

"How right you are, Roberta! A couple of angels! Yes, that's exactly what we need. I'll drink to that!"

Isy heard them **chuckling**. They clinked glasses and drank.

She turned her attention back to Amanda. "What have you got yourself involved in?" she demanded, fearing the worst. "You're not going to forge a cheque, are you?"

---

to chuckle – leise lachen

Amanda nodded. "I thought forging a signature would be easier than a Picasso," she said sarcastically.

Isy suddenly had the feeling that the restaurant was uncomfortably hot. Her blue turtleneck jumper tightened around her neck, and her ice cream tasted horribly cold. Amanda was intending to forge a cheque! It didn't bear thinking about.

"Are you crazy? What if you get caught?"

"I haven't actually done it yet, but it's only a matter of time. I don't have much choice." Amanda sounded nervous. She glanced around fearfully, reached into her bag, and pulled out a cheque. Her father's name and account details were printed on the bottom. She placed a piece of paper with a forged signature next to it. "Dad wrote the cheque for granny. I've been using it to practise." She lined up the signatures. "Can you tell the difference?"

Isy compared the two signatures and shook her head in surprise. They were identical. Amanda had a hidden talent for forgery.

"Not bad, eh?" said Amanda, licking her spoon **indulgently**.

"What do you need the money for? You've got your own account," Isy reminded her **sternly**.

"I've run out of cash," sighed Amanda. "A friend of mine was in trouble, so I lent him the money, and he hasn't paid me back. It's getting pretty des-

---

indulgent – genüsslich;
stern – streng

perate. I need the cash by the end of the month, and then Christmas is coming up..."

"What about your parents? Have you told them?"

Amanda rolled her eyes. "I'm not stupid, you know."

"Which miserable idiot won't pay the money back?"

"You don't know him," said Amanda quickly. Her face was redder than a raspberry in August.

Isy didn't believe a word of it. Judging by the colour of Amanda's cheeks, the debtor was no stranger. She waited for her friend to stop blushing. "And what about the house you went to last night?"

"That's where I'm doing a cookery course. Italian cuisine: starters, main meals and desserts!"

Amanda pointed to Signore Georgio who was solemnly slicing up a freshly-made dish of tiramisu. "He got me a special discount: four hundred euros for the whole course. He knows the chef, you see. It's a real bargain!"

"Four hundred euros?" Isy could hardly believe her ears. "Four hundred euros for a cookery course?"

They were interrupted by the sound of Amanda's mobile phone. She took it out of her bag, glanced at the number and cancelled the call. Then she turned back to Isy.

"Isy, I'm learning how to cook *panna cotta*! I'm baking *panettone*! Dad loves *panettone*. It's a Christmas present from me to him."

Isy was secretly wondering who had called Amanda's mobile. "And you want to pay for the course by forging a cheque?"

Amanda **pouted** at her **sulkily**. "How else am I supposed to come up with the cash? I talked some relatives into giving me the first hundred for the deposit. Cäsar Massimo Krause asked me to pay the rest by cheque. He's the chef, you see. He's a genius!" A smile spread over her face. "In any case, I'll have to steal a cheque from dad's chequebook. With any luck, he won't notice."

"I wouldn't count on it." Isy stared at the white tablecloth: there was a strawberry-coloured stain between their bowls. "Why haven't you tried to get a job?"

"It's easier said than done," retorted Amanda. "There are laws against schoolkids working, remember. If the job's legal, there are bound to be hundreds of applicants. I need the money urgently! I can't afford to wait around." Sighing heavily, she stuffed the cheque and the piece of paper into her pocket.

Isy's thoughts were **swirling** through her mind like confetti. She was determined to stop Amanda from committing a crime. It seemed to her that Amanda needed a job. In fact, they both needed a job: two power jobs for two power women. She had to think of something fast!

---

to pout – die Lippen trotzig vorstrecken;
sulky – schmollend;
to swirl – wirbeln

Signore Georgio was serving another round of grappa to the neighbouring table. Amanda raised her hand and made a sign. "I've told him to add the **sundaes** to dad's bill," she whispered to Isy. "He can pay for them when he's here with one of his clients."

At the table beside them, the ladies were proposing a toast. "To our angels, Roberta!"

"To our holiday angels! To some proper time off!"

They clinked glasses. Then one of them sighed. "Where are we going to find a pair of holiday angels?"

"If only I knew! We'll have to keep looking, darling."

A-ha! A thousand sparkling fireworks went off in Isy's mind. She leaned over the table, almost too excited to breathe. "That's it, Amanda! That's the solution! What do you say to a holiday-angel agency?"

"A holiday-what?"

"An agency for providing people with holiday angels! There's nothing like it on the market. And the autumn break is coming up. We'll be off school for two weeks!"

"Holiday angels?" said Amanda, puzzled. "I don't get it."

"We'll make pretty good angels, don't you think?" Isy beamed at her. "Forget all that non-

---

sundae – Eisbecher

sense about forging cheques. It's going to be heavenly. And it'll cost you three rounds of Cluedo, that's all."

– 3 –

But the German Civil Code had a thing or two to say about Isy's plan. Amanda thumped it onto Isy's desk at school the next day.

"Look, read this! We can't set up an agency, Isy! Didn't I tell you that there are laws against everything until you're eighteen? We're not allowed to say or write anything that would make people think that we're an agency."

Isy stared at the enormous book and frowned. "It wouldn't have to be official," she said defensively, pushing the volume aside. "I was thinking more along the lines of a ... *pretend* agency."

"Isy, that's even worse! We'll have the taxman and the Child Protection Agency on our backs." It was obvious that Amanda was the daughter of a successful **tax consultant**.

"OK, then we'll call it a campaign. That's it! We'll run a campaign for the duration of the school holidays and we'll call it *Making Holidays Happen*. It sounds affordable and forward-thinking. People will love it!"

"How are we ever going to get permission?"

German Civil Code – Bürgerliches Gesetzbuch;
tax consultant – Steuerberater

"Who needs permission? Amanda, stop worrying! You're driving me crazy!"

"Permission for what?" chorused Sassi and Bini, staring at them inquisitively.

"For ... Well, it's still a secret." Isy winked at them slyly. "You'll be the first to hear."

She knew right away that she couldn't keep her promise: Sassi and Bini would never learn the truth. Amanda seemed to be thinking the same. The last thing they needed was for their classmates to hear about their plan.

It was bad enough that she and Amanda were nicknamed the "calamity queens" because of the way they seemed to land themselves in trouble. Everyone knew they had a habit of getting mixed up in criminal activities – and helping to bring the **culprits** to justice. Thanks to their efforts, they had made the headlines of the local papers several times.

Their classmates took pleasure in making fun of them, partly because they were jealous of the popular pair. The pupils of 7b never tired of making jokes about "A Case for Two" and "Murder, She Wrote".

Dr Trisch, known to his pupils as "Trischi", appeared in the doorway with a stack of exercise books in his hands. "We'll talk later at my place," whispered Amanda as Trischi proceeded to inform them that their marks in the recent dictation test were shockingly low.

---

culprit – Übeltäter

The rest of the day was taken up with Biology, History and English, then Amanda and Isy were free to go home. They went straight to Amanda's place and drank green **peony** tea.

"It's really nice that you're trying to help," said Amanda after they had sat for a while **nibbling** almond cookies, listening to the Back Street Boys and gazing at a poster of Prince William. He smiled back at them shyly. "I'm not sure whether the angel idea makes sense. I mean, why would anyone go on holiday when it's rainy and cold?"

"Wake up, Amanda! The school holidays start in two weeks, remember? People go away in all kinds of weather. Pensioners are on vacation all the time!"

Shaking her head despairingly, Isy went over to Amanda's computer. "Why else would the Canary Islands and Majorca be so crowded? Think of Bad Wildbach, Bad Wörishofen and all the other **spa** resorts!"

She created a new document. "Right, I vote we focus on old people. We can offer to look after their goldfish, dogs and cacti while they're away. The next step is to design a **snazzy** flyer."

Amanda went over to the windowsill to water Aeschylus, her favourite cactus. She looked doubtfully at her friend. "Are you sure we don't need permission?"

---

peony – Pfingstrose;
to nibble – knabbern;
spa – Kurort;
snazzy – pfiffig

"We'll give each other permission, OK?" laughed Isy, her brown eyes glinting **scornfully**. "Honestly, Amanda, a moment ago you wanted to forge a cheque, and now you're scared of the slightest thing!" She reached into the biscuit tin and grabbed another cookie. "We probably shouldn't mention that we're only thirteen. It might put people off. That's not to say we're doing anything wrong – quite the opposite, in fact. We'll be freeing up our clients' time!"

"It was your idea, so you can design the flyer," said Amanda, finally giving in. "I'll cook some pasta. How about *fusilli*?"

"Fusi-what?"

"*Fusilli*! You know, like spaghetti with a perm." She ran to the kitchen and fetched a packet.

"Oh, I see," said Isy. "I thought they were called *spirelli*."

"*Spirelli*?" echoed Amanda, chuckling to herself. "Is that the Socialist word for *fusilli*? Didn't people in East Germany call anything by its proper name?"

"Don't start!" groaned Isy. "Most of the words were the same, and I've forgotten the other ones anyway. Can't we focus on making the flyer?"

"I can't think when I'm hungry," grumbled Amanda. Luckily, Isy drafted the advert in no time.

"Stuck at home with the rubber plant? Holiday cancelled because of cat & co.? We can solve your problems. The helpful staff at *Making Holidays*

---

scornful – verächtlich

Happen will take care of your loved ones while you go away. Call now and book your holiday angel."

They added the dates of the school holidays and the Schützes' telephone number at the bottom. Amanda agreed to manage the accounts. She made the international sign for money by rubbing her thumb against her index finger. "Aren't we going to tell them what it costs?"

"There'll be plenty of time to agree on a price. Let's print the adverts first."

They printed the first batch of adverts and debated what to do with them. The campaign was supposed to be a secret, so the neighbours' letterboxes were definitely **out of bounds**.

To be on the safe side, they decided to stick to districts where no one would recognize them. Fortunately, Berlin was a big city. In fact, it was huge.

In spite of reunification, Germany's capital was still divided into prosperous western districts and humbler eastern districts where widespread unemployment and modest pensions were the rule. Amanda decided that she would rather advertise her services in the west.

"I'll deliver my share in Dahlem," she said. Amanda's family came from Nuremberg in West Germany and had moved to East Berlin after her father decided to expand his accountancy business. "Everyone in Grunewald is really rich."

"If they're rich, they'll have their own staff. They won't need us," said Isy, unconvinced.

---

out of bounds – tabu

Amanda snorted. "OK, what about Wilmersdorf? It's full of widows who live off their husbands' pensions. Dad says they're a dying breed."

"In that case, you'd better hurry!" said Isy snidely. "I'll stick to East Berlin. In my opinion, East Germans deserve the occasional holiday too!"

Amanda wondered whether to **take offence**. She frowned. No one could accuse her of lacking a social conscience, but she had debts to consider. She looked at Isy accusingly and hurried into the kitchen to boil some water for the pasta. But Isy had other priorities.

"Can't you cook the fusel-thingummies another time? It's almost dark already."

Amanda looked outside and relented. She **rustled up** some salami sandwiches and they wolfed them down. Then they divided up the leaflets and hurried to the station.

Amanda travelled west to her **well-heeled** widows, while Isy headed for a nearby housing estate and stuffed her flyers into rows of grey letterboxes that were stuck like swallows' nests to the roughly plastered walls. Thirty minutes later, she delivered the last of the adverts and walked home, full of anticipation. She couldn't wait for the first client to call.

She was just unlocking the front door when the

---

to take offence – sich beleidigt fühlen;
to rustle up – schnell zubereiten;
well-heeled – betucht

telephone rang. "*Making Holidays Happen,*" she said breathlessly. "How can we help?"

"Hey, you don't need to advertise to me," said a tinny voice on the end of a mobile phone. "I was just checking to see if anyone had called."

"Yes," said Isy crossly. "You!" She slammed the phone down.

No one else called, but that was only to be expected: people were bound to need time to think about the adverts. But no one called the next day either.

Then the phone kept ringing non-stop.

A widow from Wilmersdorf wanted someone to look after her tomcat while she went on a sightseeing tour. A couple from Neukölln were taking their grandson to Florida and needed someone to take care of a canary named Fred. A husky-voiced movie director from Berlin-Mitte introduced himself as Wolfram B. Braun and requested daily deliveries of fresh bread and milk for his grandmother who would be in the apartment on her own while he worked on a shoot overseas. The shopping was to be delivered to her door by eight every morning until his return on Halloween. A student requested their help with a tortoise by the name of Leila. And two women, one from Britz and the other from Weissensee, needed someone to water the plants in their conservatories. Greenhouses were obviously **all the rage.**

---

all the rage – total »in«

Isy made a careful note of the names, addresses, dates and the nature of each request.

"We appreciate your custom," she said politely at the end of each call.

The last request that day came from a man with a friendly voice who explained that he was going away on business to the States and needed someone to look after his four-legged friend.

"It's a fabulous idea, you know," he said appreciatively. "I'm sure your holiday angels will be a great success."

"Thank you," **spluttered** Isy. She put down the receiver and had to sit down. Who would have thought that *he* of all people would call? It was a miracle that she hadn't dropped the phone.

She debated whether to call Amanda straight away or to break the news at school the next day. She decided to wait.

— 4 —

Isy was still building up to telling her friend about the phone call when Dr Trisch burst into the classroom, accompanied by a stranger whom he introduced as Detective Rose. Compared to Trischi, the detective, who was short by any standards, looked no bigger than a garden gnome. Not even the fact that he was head of the Missing Persons division at the State Investigation Bureau could add to his

---

to splutter – hastig sprechen, stottern

stature. He announced that Josepha Boskov from 7a had disappeared two days before.

"Some of you must know Josepha," said Trischi. "Has anyone seen her?"

A murmur went round the classroom, and Isy tried to remember what Josepha looked like. There were several girls from Eastern Europe in 7a and she wasn't sure which of them was Josepha. Detective Rose made a joke about his name and warned the class that he could be **prickly**, too. He showed them a photo, which was passed from hand to hand. It showed a girl whom Isy recognized because of her lively eyes.

"Look," she hissed at Amanda. "She smokes in the toilets, remember?" She raised her hand. "Amanda and I know Josepha. Have you got any leads?"

The detective shook his head and described the clothes that Josepha had been wearing on the day of her disappearance: blue Levis, a blue-grey jacket, a white sweater made by Diesel, and dark blue trainers, plus a blue-and-yellow friendship bracelet and some silver rings.

Everyone made a note of the description, then Jennifer Niemann put up her hand and asked whether Josepha had run away from home. "Maybe she had a fight with her parents," she **surmised**.

Detective Rose nodded. "Young people often go

---

prickly – stachelig;
to surmise – vermuten

missing after quarrelling with their parents, but we'd expect them to be back within a day or so. Josepha wasn't entirely happy at home. She wanted to move to Bosnia to be with her father, but her mother was given custody in Berlin. This is the fourth time that Josepha has gone missing: on the previous three occasions she was found by a police officer before she could leave the country. Her father swears that he hasn't seen her. He and Mrs Boskov are divorced, but they're talking to each other again."

Then he gave them a surprising statistic: 80,000 people went missing every year in Germany, including 8,000 in Berlin.

"I'm pleased to say that over half the cases are satisfactorily solved," said the diminutive detective. "But don't hesitate to tell us everything you know. Even the tiniest details are important."

Trischi waited for Detective Rose to leave the room, then made a final plea on Josepha's behalf. "If you want to make a statement, see me after class," he concluded. He spent the rest of the lesson trying to collect his pupils' scattered thoughts and herd them down the straight and narrow path of German grammar. When the bell rang for break time, everyone **heaved a sigh** of relief.

Of course, there was only one topic of conversation in 7b, and that was Josepha. Everyone was eager to put forward their theories.

Sassi reckoned that the missing girl had been

---

to heave a sigh – seufzen

kidnapped and was being held for **ransom** in the woods; Jennifer Niemann insisted that she had run away from home; and Bini was so distressed that she buried her face in a flowery handkerchief. Hagen Golz, also known as Gummy Bear, suspected that Josepha was dancing in a harem. "They'll like her because she's blonde," he said **bleakly**.

"Maybe we should ask the experts," drawled Tannhäuser, eyeing Isolde Schütze and Amanda Bornstein. "What do you say, ladies? Will you be solving the case?"

"I'm afraid we're too busy," said Isy coldly. And it was true. When school was over, she walked home with Amanda and told her the news.

"I can't believe it!" exclaimed Amanda, stopping mid-stride in front of a travel agency. An ancient fishing boat and lots of nets were displayed in the window as part of a promotion for holidays on the Baltic coast. "Did he recognize your voice?"

"I don't think so. He was very polite and he congratulated us on our excellent scheme. Why would he think that you and I were involved?"

"Because he's a crime writer."

"That doesn't mean he knows everything."

"It hasn't stopped him **rumbling** us before," sighed Amanda.

She was right. Mr Rimpau had Argus eyes. In fact, he probably had x-ray vision as well. They had

---

ransom – Lösegeld;
bleak – freudlos;
to rumble s.o. – jmdn. ertappen

been introduced to the crime writer and his cute dog Alfredo in Altgrünheide last year. Their first meeting had been **marred** by a few unfortunate mix-ups and they had suspected the kind-hearted and helpful Mr Rimpau of being a thief. Thankfully, he had forgiven them and become their loyal friend. Last spring when they were chasing a gang of criminals at Berlin zoo, Mr Rimpau had rescued them from all kinds of difficulties, and they were eternally grateful for his help. But his unexpected interest in their project was anything but a welcome surprise. He was bound to ruin everything, not least because he always saw dangers that didn't exist. Perhaps it was a consequence of writing about crime.

Amanda thought for a moment. "Why does he want a holiday angel?"

"He needs someone to look after Alfredo while he flies to the States."

"He wants us to look after his dog?" Amanda stared at her, aghast. "Tell me you said no!"

"How was I supposed to refuse? And anyway, it won't be a problem: Alfredo can stay with me."

"We haven't even started and already we're in trouble!" wailed Amanda. They walked in silence for a while. It was obvious that there was no right decision: on the one hand, they couldn't **leave** Alfredo **in the lurch**; on the other, they couldn't risk Mr Rimpau ruining their campaign.

---

to mar – beeinträchtigen, verderben;
to leave s.o. in the lurch – jmdn. im Stich lassen

Their spirits sank.

"How about disguising ourselves?" suggested Amanda with a crafty smile. "With good enough costumes, even Mr Argus-Eyes won't recognize us."

Isy brightened up. It seemed to her that the plan might work. "OK, you buy the outfits, but don't spend too much!" she said sternly. She hurried off and took the shortest route home, hoping to arrive before Benedikt. Isy couldn't leave the telephone unattended when the rest of her family was around. Luckily her parents worked full-time: her mother had found a proper job in spring.

She got to the apartment first, poured some milk for Selma, and then the phone rang. It was a grammar school teacher by the name of Mrs Ober-Lippe calling to say that she wanted to enrol for a language course in London and needed a holiday angel to empty her mailbox. She was particularly concerned about the junk mail and flyers.

"No problem, we'll take care of it," promised Isy. "Thank you for your custom."

She sat down to do her homework. Once or twice she found herself thinking about the missing Josepha, whose disappearance had caused such a stir. Maybe Jennifer Niemann was right, and she had quarrelled with her mother. Isy pictured Josepha as a runaway and remembered the cheeky sparkle in her eyes. There was something about them that reminded Isy of a blackbird.

She had ploughed through most of her homework when someone rang the doorbell and kept their finger on the buzzer. Isy assumed that it was one of Benedikt's friends. They always rang the bell as if their lives depended on it.

"He's not in!" she yelled, but the noise didn't stop. In the end she **yanked** open the door and froze. She could scarcely believe her eyes.

Standing on the doorstep was a **plump** woman with curly blonde hair. She was wearing a shiny gold headband and plastic glasses with blue tinted lenses. Her cheeks were bright red and her film-star lips were the colour of cherries. A long cape of fluffy white fleece was draped across her shoulders.

"What are you staring at?" said the strange woman in Amanda's voice. "I disguised myself as a holiday angel like we agreed. The saleswoman said I looked an absolute scream."

Isy couldn't help thinking that the saleswoman was right: the sight of the holiday angel was enough to make anyone scream. She stood back **glumly** to let her friend come in. Mr Rimpau would have to be **clairvoyant** to see through a disguise like that. Amanda looked at her triumphantly and handed her a bag. "The wigs were from Aldi, the glasses from Drospa, and the capes from Kaufhof. You can't get cheaper than that!"

She took off her cape and sat down on Isy's couch.

---

to yank – heftig an etwas ziehen;
plump – pummelig;
glum – verdrossen, missmutig;
clairvoyant – hellseherisch

"It's awfully cramped in here," she said as usual. "I don't know how you put up with such a tiny room."

"I'd rather have a tiny room than no room at all," retorted Isy. Amanda knew perfectly well that there were only two proper bedrooms in the apartment: one for her parents, and the other for Benedikt. She had to make do with a room the size of a broom cupboard, but at least she had it to herself.

"Would you like a drink?"

"Guava juice, please." Amanda took a careful look at the list of addresses and requests while Isy went into the kitchen to pour two glasses of chilled lemonade.

Whatever guava juice was, the Schützes certainly didn't have any. They weren't in a tropical rainforest, after all!

"This is all we've got, I'm afraid," she said, handing her a glass of **fizzy pop**.

"Not to worry," murmured Amanda. "Do you think fourteen clients will be enough?"

"We can probably manage one more. And we'll start as soon as school breaks up."

As if by magic, the telephone rang.

"I'll answer it," volunteered Amanda, running into the hall. Her friend heard her say, "*Making Holidays Happen*! How can I help you?"

Isy smiled to herself and folded the client list carefully. Suddenly Amanda's pink mobile phone

---

fizzy pop – Limonade mit viel Kohlensäure

began to beep. Isy hesitated for a moment. It was rude to read other people's text messages – but she couldn't resist the temptation. She picked up the mobile from the couch. The text was to a certain **"Bumblebee"** and was sent from someone who promised to come up with the **"dough"**. It concluded with the line "Have I ever let you down?" and was signed "Ru".

Isy didn't need to check the list of contacts on Amanda's phone. The mysterious "Ru" could only be one person: Ruky König from Altgrünheide, the good-looking half-Cuban with black braids who played Mozart to his vegetables and went for joyrides in other people's cars. It was strange that Amanda had wanted to keep his identity a secret. Isy had never heard her friend referred to as "Bumblebee". Her thoughts were interrupted when Amanda **buzzed** back into the room.

"It was a Mrs von Leinungen from Charlottenburg. She wants to go away with her bridge club and she needs someone to look after two cats and a myrtle plant. The cats only eat Chinese."

Isy blinked in astonishment. "You're joking! What did you say?"

Amanda grinned. "I told her to leave it to us. I said we'd do anything – with the exception of belly dancing."

---

bumblebee – Hummel;
dough – Knete;
buzz – schwirren

— 5 —

During the final period of the first school day that week Isy shuffled nervously on her seat. She kept glancing at the clock while their new biology teacher tried to interest them in the largest **gland** in the human body: the liver.

On Sunday, Isy's mum had cooked liver and onions for dinner when Amanda had come round to play three games of Cluedo as promised. After the fiasco with Mrs Peacock, Amanda had chosen to be Mrs White, the housekeeper in charge of the black-and-white **tiled** kitchen.

Once again, Amanda was charmed by the beautiful English mansion and wandered starry-eyed through the elegant rooms, venturing into underground passageways and making all kinds of **outrageous** accusations. By the end of the third game, she couldn't honesty describe herself as a Cluedo fan, but her victory in the final round certainly helped to improve her mood.

Now she and Isy were counting the minutes. Just as the bell rang, Detective Rose pushed his way into the room. The prickly detective held up a photograph of Mirko Boskov. His ex-wife suspected him of hiding their daughter somewhere in Bosnia. According to her, he had collected Josepha from school in his white Corsa and taken her home with

---

gland – Drüse;
tiled – gekachelt;
outrageous – unerhört

him. Mr Boskov was on his way to Berlin to **refute** the allegations in person.

"Quiet please," shouted the detective, trying to restore order. "Did anyone see Mr Boskov in a white Corsa near the school?"

Isy and Amanda glanced at the photo and shook their heads simultaneously. Then they ran home, pulled on their wigs, put on their blue-tinted glasses and threw on their capes. They hoped to goodness that none of their schoolmates would see them. After a final glance in the mirror, they were ready to leave.

Their first client that afternoon was Mrs von Leinungen from Charlottenburg whose cats only ate Chinese.

"Do you think they use **chopsticks**?" whispered Isy as they rang the brass doorbell and waited in the carpeted corridor of an elegant apartment block.

"*Making Holidays Happen,*" they chorused when a fragile, white-haired lady **peered** through the door. "We're your holiday angels."

"Come in," said the old lady, ushering them into the sunny apartment that she shared with her **feline** companions, Ottilie and Charlotte.

To Isy's surprise, the pets weren't posh pedigree cats, but normal black-and-white **moggies** like Selma.

---

refute – widerlegen;
chopsticks – Essstäbchen; to peer – blicken;
feline – Katzen; moggy *(slang)* – Katze

Amanda got straight to the point. "Isn't it a bit odd for cats to eat Chinese?" she asked. She and Isy were sitting on Mrs von Leinungen's silk-covered period furniture, drinking tea from fine china cups and nibbling fruitcake. "Are they spoilt?"

Mrs von Leinungen wiped a few crumbs from the otherwise spotless white tablecloth and shook her head. "Not at all. Otti and Lotti were born near a Chinese restaurant. Their mother fed them from … She fed them from the dustbins, I'm afraid."

"There's no need to apologize, I was practically raised on Chinese! Not like poor Isy – there weren't any Chinese takeaways in East Berlin."

"There weren't any tax consultants either," said Isy **scornfully**. "That's why your father is **making such a killing**."

Mrs von Leinungen chuckled. "An East-West alliance, I see."

Amanda nodded. "We're the perfect team!" she said proudly, smiling at their host. "Don't you worry, Mrs von Leinungen. You can enjoy your holiday in the knowledge that your cats are being well fed. I'll cook them chop suey and spring rolls and won-tons! You'll be able to hear them purring from here to Beijing." She was about to **regale** Otti and Lotti's owner with a list of Chinese specialities, when the telephone rang.

---

scornful – spöttisch;
to make a killing – absahnen;
regale – bewirten

"That's wonderful, dear. If only I could trust my nephew to take such good care of my cats!" Mrs von Leinungen got up from the sofa and made her way to the next room to answer the call. A moment later, she was back. "They rang off as soon as I picked the phone up. It's been going on for days." She laughed nervously. "They want to know if I've left already. My relatives are awfully nosey."

"What makes you think it's your relatives?" asked Isy. "Someone else might be after you."

"Only the taxman," **quipped** Mrs von Leinungen. They all laughed.

"Joking aside, I'm almost certain that someone's been coming into my apartment while I'm out." The elderly lady smoothed the tablecloth anxiously. "I haven't been to the police. Those young officers think old girls like me are all dotty …"

"Is anything missing?" asked Isy, her curiosity aroused. "Have you checked your belongings?"

Mrs von Leinungen nodded. "Everything's here."

Isy frowned. "Then how do you know someone was in the apartment?"

Mrs von Leinungen pointed to an armchair by the window. It was upholstered in beautiful Gobelin tapestry. "The chair was too far to the right. Someone had moved it." She looked at Isy with the stubbornness of an old person who was convinced that she was right. "I never move that armchair. It's always in exactly the same place."

---

to quip – witzeln

She stood up abruptly to signal that the matter was closed. "In the event of an emergency, you can contact me at the club," she said. She wrote down the address and left it on her **bureau**.

Then she showed them the litter tray, the eternally thirsty myrtle plant, and the immaculately tidy kitchen. Amanda lost no time in inspecting the wok and the Chinese spices, while Isy explained their terms and conditions.

"You'll have to cover the cost of the food and any other expenses," she concluded. "Oh, and we can give you a ten per cent discount if you pay cash."

The old woman whistled through her false teeth. "That's what I call professional service," she said, impressed.

"A ten percent discount?" protested Amanda twenty minutes later when they found themselves a seat on the bus. The other passengers were staring at them curiously. "I'm not Mother Theresa, you know! Mrs von Leinungen's teacups were Meissen china!"

"So what? We're not a proper agency, remember! We can't exactly ask her to write us a cheque."

Isy's words had little effect on Amanda, who went into a **sulk** and didn't stop pouting until they were on the doorstep of the student with the tortoise.

He introduced himself as Max and welcomed

---

bureau – Schreibtisch;
to sulk – schmollen

them like old friends. He had a **beguiling** smile. His apartment wouldn't have been bad either, if he bothered to tidy it up. They made their way **valiantly** past stacks of magazines, empty beer cans, books and stray black socks. At last they reached the glass terrarium, but Leila wasn't home. Like others of her species, she preferred to spend the day in the one-room apartment of her **mottled** brown shell.

"Take a seat," said Max, pointing to the assortment of chairs grouped around the large round table. He told them that he was feeling down because his girlfriend had left him. To make matters worse, he was worried about Leila. According to the vet, she needed vitamin drops and fresh lettuce every morning. The trouble was, he was supposed to be working as an intern in Leipzig for two weeks. He would have called his tutor and cancelled, but the holiday angels' flyer had arrived just in time. Beaming, he poured three tumblers of red wine. "You're a **godsend**," he told them. "Do you do a student discount?"

To Isy's horror, her friend nodded and tipped the red wine down her throat. It was always the same with Amanda. As soon as she was in the presence of a good-looking guy, she acted up terribly. Isy half expected her to ask for a cigarette.

---

to beguile – verführen;
valiant – tapfer;
mottled – meliert;
to be a godsend – wie gerufen kommen

"Can I borrow a cigarette?" purred Amanda, right on cue. Isy stood up before Max had time to answer. "I'm afraid we're in a hurry. Our clients are waiting."

"Are you crazy?" hissed Amanda as soon as they were out of the door. "Why did you have to rush out like that? There's no need to be so rude!"

"Oh really? I was worried what kind of discount you might offer him next!" snapped Isy. "Honestly, Amanda, you should have asked me first."

"You can't expect me to ask you about every stupid detail!"

"Stupid detail? OK, fine! You can spend the next two weeks feeding his tortoise for nothing, if you like. I'm not the one who needs the cash!"

The argument would have continued for a while longer, if Amanda hadn't been distracted by the world's largest pumpkin. She stared wide-eyed at the record-breaking vegetable.

"How much does it weigh?" she asked the Turkish stallholder.

He stared back at her in surprise. Angels clearly didn't figure among his usual clientele. He heaved the pumpkin onto an ancient set of scales and waited for the arrow to settle. It weighed six whole kilos.

"That's twelve pounds," gasped Isy.

"Excellent, I'll take it," said Amanda.

Isy was starting to question the sanity of her friend. What on earth did she want with such an enormous pumpkin? To her astonishment, Amanda paid the full price and clasped the huge, round vegetable in her arms.

Shaking her head incredulously, Isy set off down the street. It seemed to her that Amanda was paying the penalty for **guzzling** a whole tumbler of red wine. She decided to leave her friend to it. Amanda would only have herself to blame if her arms dropped off; Isy had no intention of lifting a finger to help her. If her friend was hoping that Isy would offer to carry it for her, she was very much mistaken.

"Do you want a hand with that?" offered Isy a moment later. She took the pumpkin from her exhausted friend. "I don't understand why you bought it. Halloween isn't for another three weeks."

"Who said anything about Halloween? I'm going to turn it into pumpkin pie. Pio promised to demonstrate the recipe on his show next week."

Renowned TV chef Professor Pioschleck was Amanda's guru. On one occasion, she had woken up, convinced that he had invited her onto his programme, but it was only a dream: Pio's guests were always famous. But Amanda was a natural in the kitchen, and Isy credited herself with discovering her talent: before their trip to Altgrünheide, Amanda hadn't realized that she could cook.

They carried the pumpkin heroically through the streets of Berlin, feeling rather like Atlas carrying the globe. At last they reached Mr Rimpau's

---

to guzzle – gierig trinken

apartment block. They left the pumpkin in the entrance hall.

"What if someone steals it?"

"No one's going to steal a pumpkin!"

"They'd better not," threatened Amanda, pulling her wig nervously over her forehead. "Can you tell it's me?"

"Only because of your rolling "*r*". You'll be fine if you keep your mouth shut."

Amanda had no problem with that, and so it was decided that Isy would communicate in broken German with Mr Rimpau, while her companion kept quiet. With any luck, he would think they were foreigners.

"Just relax," said Isy. "Imagine you're sipping tea with Prince William in Buckingham Palace, and it won't be so bad."

Amanda opened her mouth to say something, but her mobile rang instead.

"For goodness sake, turn it off!" hissed Isy. "You'll ruin everything!"

The **jittery** Amanda turned off her phone while Isy rang the bell. She still had her finger on the buzzer when Mr Rimpau flung open the door. He peered at them quizzically over his pipe. Isy guessed that he hadn't pictured his holiday angels quite like this.

"Hello," he said uncertainly.

"Hello," they murmured, following him down

---

jittery (slang) – ängstlich

the familiar corridor past floor-to-ceiling shelves of books.

He stopped outside his study and glanced at their capes. "Can I relieve you of your wings?"

Amanda started to giggle, but was silenced by a warning glance from Isy, who didn't want Mr Rimpau to recognize her laugh.

They stepped into the author's hallowed workplace. Pale afternoon sun slanted across the burgundy carpet, illuminating his dark wooden desk. Isy couldn't help wondering whether Amanda was still under the influence of the tumbler of red wine. She glanced at her **warily** from the corner of her eye.

Amanda looked incredibly tense. She was sitting next to Mr Rimpau, pretending not to understand anything that he said.

"Do you speak English? French? Italian?"

Amanda kept her nerve. She shook her head mutely.

"I see. So you speak an unknown language, then." The writer smiled kindly. "And by the looks of your outfit, you're from another galaxy. Well, not to worry. The character that you'll be taking care of speaks a different dialect as well, but I'm sure you'll understand each other. He speaks from the heart – from a **canine** heart, to be precise." He got up to open the tinted glass door to the adjacent room.

---

wary – behutsam, vorsichtig;
canine – Hund

It was only then that Isy realized that she and Amanda had forgotten a very important detail. Mr Rimpau pushed down the handle, and a medium-sized, grey-coated dog charged into the study. Alfredo threw himself on Isy, licking her excitedly. Isy's cheeks flushed so red that she buried her face in his fur.

A tense silence descended on the room, then Mr Rimpau said soberly, "You can fool a **gullible** human, but not a clever dog. Good work, Alfredo!"

— 6 —

"**You total idiot**!" raged Isy. "You complete and utter **wally**!"

It was midnight and Isy was cursing herself furiously.

She couldn't get to sleep, not after she had made such a fool of herself. To think that she had forgotten the legendary power of the canine nose!

If only they had spent less time worrying about Mr Rimpau, they might have realized that blonde wigs and blue glasses would never fool a schnauzer.

Besides, Alfredo was a personal friend. They had known him since last October when they first met Mr Rimpau in Altgrünheide. Isy had never suspected that his affection would land them in such a mess.

---

gullible – leichtgläubig;
wally (slang) – blöde Gans

Their reaction to the crisis had undoubtedly made things worse.

She and Amanda had been too shocked, ashamed and embarrassed to say another word. In their haste to leave, they had fled the study, the apartment, and the building without stopping to collect the pumpkin from the hall.

It was a while before they recovered their breath, but then they discussed what had happened.

"You really messed things up," said Amanda, still **wheezing**.

"I don't see why you're blaming me!"

"You should have remembered how much Alfredo likes you! He didn't jump up and down at the sight of me!"

There was no faulting Amanda's logic, and the **crestfallen** pair had made their way home.

Hours later, Isy was still tossing and turning in bed. She was so embarrassed by it all. They would have to apologize, but she wasn't sure how. Would Mr Rimpau prefer flowers, a letter or a meal? Isy decided that Amanda should cook for Alfredo and his owner. Mr Rimpau would surely be **mollified** by her culinary expertise. And what was the point of paying for an expensive cookery course if she couldn't put her talents to good use? She decided to ask her friend the next morning at school. The thought of appeasing Mr Rimpau with a home-

---

to wheeze – keuchen;
crestfallen – niedergeschlagen;
to mollify – besänftigen

cooked dinner was so soothing that she finally fell asleep.

The next morning, the streets were covered in shimmering frost and the dank air felt bitterly cold against her skin. She waited for Amanda under the three small maple trees in front of the supermarket and was surprised to see the dark rings around her eyes. Amanda had slept badly as well. She was still **mourning** the loss of her record-breaking vegetable. "I'll never get hold of such an amazing pumpkin again."

"I'll buy you another one," promised Isy, "but only if you cook a special dinner for Mr Rimpau and Alfredo."

Amanda groaned. "I don't think I'm ready to see Mr Rimpau again," she confessed.

"It can wait a few days," Isy **reassured** her. "We'll have to explain things somehow. And anyhow, he still needs someone to look after Alfredo when he flies to New York."

"Guardian angels for a schnauzer," snorted Amanda, laughing in spite of herself.

There wasn't much else to laugh about that morning.

The school day began with an impossibly difficult maths test. Next came a lesson with a student teacher, and then Detective Rose made his third appearance in Trischi's class. Isy was so tired of the sight of him that she nearly groaned out loud when

---

to mourn – trauern;
to reassure – beruhigen

he walked through the door. It was definitely time for the holidays.

According to Detective Rose, three teams of police dogs were **scouring** the woods for Josepha, but the focus of the investigation was a pupil from the ninth grade who had supposedly been involved with the missing girl. The blue-and-yellow friendship bracelet belonged to him. Detective Rose handed around a photo.

Most of the class knew the ninth-grader by sight. He was tall, muscular and good-looking. Isy recognized him at once: she and Amanda were always bumping into him at school. His name was Janho. But they had never seen him with Josepha. She would have remembered a thing like that.

"What do you mean, *involved*?" asked Isy.

The detective stroked his hat. "Well, er… To be honest, we're still looking into it."

Isy couldn't believe the **cheek** of the man. There was nothing honest about an answer like that! She glanced at Tannhäuser and Gummy Bear who were exchanging knowing looks.

"What are you smiling at?" she whispered. "Is there something you're not telling?"

"Come on, Isy, everyone knows."

"Everyone knows what?"

"That Janho has a thing for party pills," growled Gummy Bear irritably.

---

to scour – *(hier)* gründlich durchsuchen;
cheek – *(hier)* Frechheit

"Party pills?" echoed Amanda, puzzled, when Isy told her the news. They had struggled through the final period and were sitting in the warmth of the Berlin metro, looking out from under their blonde wigs and surveying their surroundings through blue-tinted lenses. "Do you mean drugs?"

"I don't suppose he's addicted to Smarties," retorted Isy, who could tell that her friend was shocked. Hardly a day went by without a news item or a newspaper article on drug abuse, but they had never suspected that any of their schoolmates would be involved. Had someone been taking drugs in their school? More to the point, had someone been taking drugs in classroom 7a? It was an uncomfortable thought.

It was almost as uncomfortable as meeting Mrs Ober-Lippe, the grammar school teacher who had booked a language course in London. Instead of inviting them into her apartment, their new client made them stand in the hallway while she lectured them about burglars, who were drawn like magnets to overflowing mailboxes. At last, and with some reluctance, she handed them her keys. They made their escape under the suspicious glare of her bespectacled eyes.

"I don't think she likes us," observed Amanda with a grin. She looked up the next address on her map. The client was called Helga Wulf and her straw-coloured hair was piled up like a **haystack** on

---

haystack – Heuhaufen

her head. Her cheeks were covered in bright pink blusher. She giggled when she saw their outfits and asked them to prove their identity. "What's the name of your agency? *Heavenly Help*?"

"We're not from an agency. *Making Holidays Happen* is a special campaign to coincide with the school break."

"Goodness me," trilled Mrs Wulf. "I'll call a proper agency, thank you very much." She shut the door quickly.

They never heard from her again.

The next few clients were more broad-minded, especially when they heard about the discounts on offer.

"What did I tell you?" grumbled Amanda, stepping into the elevator that would take them to the final client on their list. "We're not charging enough. They'd easily pay more…"

"Sure," said Isy. "But if we charged more, they'd ask more questions." She pressed the button for the eleventh storey. "What if everyone reacted like Miss Marple-Wulf? We've been exceptionally lucky."

They waited on the green doormat of apartment 1101. A moment later, as they looked into the eagle eyes of the movie director, Isy had a feeling that their luck was about to run out. Her instincts told her that Wolfram B. Braun was a troublemaker. There was nothing actually wrong with him, and Amanda was bound to make fun of her for suspecting such a well-mannered, well-dressed man. He was in his early forties, with tanned skin and a

husky voice. No one who met him would doubt his affection for his grandmother or his passion for his work – except Isy, of course.

"Have you ever filmed in Hollywood?" asked Amanda, hanging on his every word. Wolfram B. Braun looked at her from his black leather director's chair and nodded. She almost fell off her seat. "Have you worked with Brad Pitt?"

"I've worked with Maximilian Schell," he boasted.

"Is he famous?"

"Ten times more famous than Brad Pitt!"

For a moment Amanda **wavered**, unable to imagine anyone more famous than Brad Pitt. She decided to believe him, and smiled. "I bet you're a brilliant director, Mr Braun."

*She's **buttering him up***, thought Isy. Amanda had always dreamt of a career in films.

Meanwhile, Isy was scanning the room. It wasn't how she had imagined a movie director's apartment. The glossy magazines always showed pictures of luxurious mansions with spa pools, never-ending pastel-coloured sofas and marble fireplaces.

The furniture in Mr Braun's apartment didn't match. He didn't have any artwork, **let alone** a fancy fireplace. The rooms were curiously empty,

---

husky – rau, heiser;
to waver – zaudern;
to butter s.o. up – jmdm. schmeicheln;
let alone – geschweige denn

as if Mr Braun and his grandmother were in the process of moving out. Amanda was lolling on an elegant green Art Nouveau sofa, but it was stranded forlornly in the middle of the room.

Isy rested the notepad on her knee and re-read the entry. Next to the director's name was written: *six bread rolls and a bottle of milk to be delivered by eight in the morning at the latest!* She had underlined the next sentence: *hang the shopping on the front door and DON'T knock – Mr Braun's grandma will be asleep*.

"Anything else you'd like us to do?"

"We're lucky enough to have a very kind neighbour who visits her in the afternoon. She'll be well looked after – but you could always challenge her to a game of bridge."

Isy couldn't understand the attraction of the game.

"I'm afraid we don't know how."

"What kind of games do you play?"

"Trivial Pursuit or Cluedo. I love Cluedo!"

The director looked down his nose at her. "Cluedo? How childish!"

Isy could feel herself blushing with embarrassment. "Six bread rolls and a bottle of milk every morning," she said briskly. "We'll need cash payment in advance. That's forty euros including the shopping."

"Does your grandma really eat six bread rolls for breakfast?" asked Amanda nosily.

Wolfram B. Braun whipped out his wallet. "She dunks them in a bowl of milk and honey. It keeps her happy all day." He smiled indulgently and fished out a couple of notes. The powerful beam of the desk lamp made his dark hair shimmer with a hint of red. Isy couldn't understand why it was always so obvious when men dyed their hair. Mr Braun wasn't even especially old. She accepted the notes, and Mr Braun patted his watch anxiously. "Grandma will be waiting at the physiotherapist's. I'm afraid I'll have to **dash**."

"No problem," said Amanda, leaping up from the sofa. "We'll leave you in peace."

"Actually," Isy contradicted her, "there is a problem. Where's the rest of the cash?"

She held out her hand so that her friend could see what was wrong. Amanda gasped: Mr Braun had given them barely half of the money that they had asked for. It was just as well that Isy had checked. Amanda glared at him indignantly. "Is this some kind of joke?"

"Apparently so," he said, stroking his yellow silk cravat. "I refuse **to be strung along** by a couple of actresses." He laughed **hoarsely**. "Surely you didn't think you could fool a professional like me?"

---

to dash – sich sputen;
to be strung along – hinters Licht geführt werden;
hoarse – heiser

– 7 –

Amanda and Isy had been outsmarted.

They beat a hasty retreat. Still feeling shocked and dazed, they quickly changed into their normal clothes and rushed to Georgio's. Sighing, they **devoured** a portion of delectable strawberry ice cream. They needed time to recover from their latest **setback**.

"And he seemed so nice at first," muttered Amanda, still upset.

"Not to me, he didn't," said Isy grimly. "I knew he was a troublemaker."

"Really?" Amanda sighed. "The worst thing is, he was right about us!"

Isy nodded sadly. From the corner of her eye she spotted Signore Georgio walking towards them with a tray of goodies. She wondered which table they were for.

"With the compliments of the chef!" Georgio beamed at them. "A little something to warm up your stomachs after all that ice cream!"

A moment later, they were feasting their eyes on bowls of shiny olives, spicy slices of sizzling pizza, and delicate balls of mozzarella cheese.

"Grazie! Fantastico! Mille, mille baci!" exclaimed Amanda, blowing Georgio a kiss. She shoved a slice of pizza greedily into her mouth. Sometimes Isy was swept away by her enthusiasm.

---

to devour – verschlingen;
setback – Rückschlag

She was proud to know someone who could babble away in Italian, pick through racks of expensive designer clothes, and dissect a **lobster** without making a mess. Of course, Amanda could also be frustratingly lazy and stubborn, but she made up for it by leaving the decisions to her more ambitious and adaptable friend. Who else would allow themselves to be bossed about like that? Perhaps that was the key to their friendship: they didn't tread on each other's toes. Their talents lay in different directions, so there was never any rivalry between them.

The two friends **tucked into** the Italian treats, and Isy's thoughts returned to the director.

He had laughed in their faces while they trembled like **startled** rabbits. After that, he had redeemed himself a little by offering them a deal: if they completed the job to his satisfaction, he would pay them the rest of the money and some extra at the end. Isy wasn't prepared to forgive him for his behaviour: what kind of person didn't like Cluedo?

"Let's take Werner B. Braun off our list," she suggested. "For all I care, he can order his grandma's shopping direct from the Heavenly Spirit."

"But he's a movie director! We need contacts like that!"

Isy snorted contemptuously. "Speak for yourself! I don't want to be discovered."

---

lobster – Hummer;
to tuck into – tüchtig zugreifen;
to startle – erschrecken

"Well, I do!" said Amanda, dropping a grey olive stone onto her plate.

That evening they went their separate ways. Amanda hurried to her cookery class, while Isy tried to get home in time for dinner. Her parents were becoming suspicious.

"Is there something you're not telling us?" enquired her mother as soon as she walked through the door. Mrs Schütze was tired of reading about her daughter's exploits in the newspapers; if Isy was tracking a criminal, she wanted to hear about it firsthand. She pointed to the red telephone in the hallway. "Someone called and asked for a holiday angel."

"A holiday angel?" chuckled Isy. "What a **weird** idea!"

"Especially since he seemed to think our telephone number was printed on a flyer. He found it in his mailbox. He mentioned a campaign – *Making Holidays Happen,* or something. According to Benedikt, it wasn't the first funny phone call." Her mother sighed deeply. "If you're up to something, you'd better tell me now, Isolde. And don't forget to tidy your room!"

"I'm not up to anything!" protested Isy, doing her best to sound **indignant**.

Later that evening, while they were watching the news, Isy came under fire from her parents

---

weird – seltsam, abartig;
indignant – empört

again. A reporter had just finished describing how Tornado jets were using heat-seeking technology to search for Josepha. The picture cut to an interview with the distraught Mrs Boskov. She had spoken to her husband and withdrawn her accusation.

"Josepha goes to your school, doesn't she? You're not interfering with the investigation, are you, Isolde? Leave it to the experts. The police will find her soon enough."

"I haven't been interfering with anything," protested Isy, and this time it was true.

All the same, it was **disconcerting** to know that her parents had **smelt a rat**. She slipped out of bed to call Amanda's mobile.

"My parents are getting suspicious! We'll have to abandon the campaign!" she warned Amanda.

"Is that why you're calling in the middle of the night?" her friend said irritably.

"In the middle of the night? It's not even nine o'clock!"

"So what? I'm tired! You're always such a drama queen!"

"A drama queen? You're the drama queen, Amanda! If it weren't for you, my life would be easy," she said accusingly and slammed down the phone. *Not a word of thanks! How typical of Amanda!* Isy was tempted to leave her friend to deal with her problems on her own. There was simply no helping some people. She could think of bet-

---

disconcerting – beunruhigend;
to smell a rat – Verdacht schöpfen

ter things to do with her holidays than empty other people's mailboxes, feed their cats and water their rubber plants.

She stormed back to bed and stared into the darkness. In her mind's eye she saw a series of snapshots: memories of good and bad times with Amanda.

Sometimes Amanda was really cool, like the time in Altgrünheide when she buried the thief's mask under a pile of steaming spaghetti and hid it in the freezer as **evidence** . Or when she hid under the Königs' flowery sofa and stared at the **intruder's** feet.

Isy could still remember the mouth-watering smell of the risotto that Amanda had cooked for a genuine thief and mistakenly served to an innocent man. She paled as she recalled how they had unwittingly walked out of Berlin zoo on Easter Sunday with a clutch of precious Peregrine falcon eggs that a smuggler had stolen for an oil sheikh.

Amanda had been kidnapped, and Isy had rushed to her aid without a thought for her own safety. She knew that Amanda would have done the same for her. They had stuck by each other through thick and thin. So what if Amanda had refused to tell her that Ruky had borrowed the money! She could keep it a secret for the next fifty years if she liked. When the holidays started, Isy would be flitting through the streets, carrying out her duty as a holi-

---

evidence – Beweismittel;
intruder – Eindringling

day angel, not lying cosily in bed. Her priority was to put a stop to the phone calls before her parents put a stop to their campaign.

In the final week of school Isy made a **concerted** effort to silence the red telephone in the hall. She and Amanda equipped themselves with screwdrivers and **pliers** and fiddled with the mysterious tangle of wires until they were convinced they had found the right one. A moment later, the phone fought back by ringing loudly and a Mrs Knosalla from Berlin-Karlshorst demanded to speak to a holiday angel.

"I'm terribly sorry, but we're completely booked," said Isy truthfully. "The campaign is oversubscribed. I'm afraid we can't help you."

"What do you mean, can't help me?" screeched the woman. "First you block my mailbox with your flyer, and then you turn your back on me! Is it because I'm East German?"

"I'm East German, too," said Isy, who couldn't make sense of the woman's logic. "What seems to be the problem?"

"The problem? The problem is that I'm being treated like a second-class citizen! Don't you know what it's like to lose your job, be forced to give up your home, and live off the dole?"

"Oh," said Isy nervously, "I meant: what would you like us to do?"

---

concerted – gezielt, entschlossen;
pliers *(pl.)* – Zange

"I need someone to look after Gottfried," wailed the woman, trying not to sob. "They don't allow Japanese goldfish at the beauty spa. I won the holiday in a competition. It's the prize of a lifetime!"

"All right then," conceded Isy, ignoring Amanda's angry glares. "We'll make an exception."

The telephone kept ringing. Holiday angels were obviously in demand. Isy and Amanda put up with the noise for two painful afternoons, but the next day they picked up the **tinkling** telephone and hurled it furiously against the floor. It was the last they heard from it.

On the fourth day the headmaster paid a visit to 7b. Someone had written "Rose on the Scent" on the board. The school was organizing a publicity campaign to highlight Josepha's disappearance and the pupils were expected to sacrifice a day of their holidays in order to hand out pictures of the missing girl. Everyone agreed to participate, with the exception of Jennifer Niemann, who proudly announced that she would be sunning herself in the Dominican Republic.

And on the fifth day, they left the classroom for two precious weeks of holiday. The holiday angels could get to work!

---

to tinkle – klingeln, bimmeln

— 8 —

They started that very afternoon. Their first priority was to apologize to Mr Rimpau. They went round to say sorry and invite him to a special meal.

"Nothing's too much trouble," said Amanda generously. "Just tell me what you'd like."

Unfortunately, what Mr Rimpau wanted was for them to abandon their campaign.

"But all those people are relying on us," protested Isy. She **jingled** their bag of keys. "We can't let them down!"

"Think of the risk! You shouldn't be going into strangers' houses on your own," said Mr Rimpau sternly. He mixed himself a whisky on the rocks. "Have you told your parents what you're up to?"

"They know we're doing odd jobs to raise a bit of cash," replied Amanda in a small voice.

"Can't you find another way of earning money?"

"I'm afraid not, Mr Rimpau. Amanda tried everything!" said Isy, sipping a mug of their host's best tea. It tasted pleasantly of cinnamon. A few moments earlier, they had accompanied Mr Rimpau to the kitchen and waited for the kettle to boil. Isy and Amanda's attention had been drawn to a collection of **preserving jars** that were cooling on a checked cloth. The jars were filled with golden chunks of pumpkin.

---

to jingle – klimpern;
preserving jar – Einweckglas

Isy and Amanda had stared and stared. On seeing their **dumbfounded** expressions, Mr Rimpau had chuckled. "Someone left a pumpkin by our door. A real whopper!" He threw up his hands to indicate the girth of the incredible vegetable. It was the size of Amanda's record-breaking pumpkin. "My wife chopped it up and made some sweet-and-sour chutney before she flew to Rome. Everyone in the apartment block will get their own jar."

"I hope they like it!" said Amanda with a sweet-and-sour smile to match the chutney.

Now they were relaxing in the lounge while Mr Rimpau packed his hand luggage. Alfredo had stretched out on the rug and was enjoying being tickled.

"I wish you wouldn't drag me into your exploits," the writer grumbled crossly. "You've put my nerves under enough strain already. I'm supposed to be meeting my publishers in New York. I don't want to be worrying about the **reckless** adventures of a couple of teenage girls!"

"There's nothing to worry about!" declared Isy, rushing to reassure him. "It's perfectly safe. The owners will be on holiday, their flats will be empty, and it won't be the least bit dangerous – unless we get pricked by a cactus!"

"I hope you're right," said the author in a strict voice. He pointed to his dog. "I want you to take Alfredo with you wherever you go. He'll accompany

---

dumbfounded – verblüfft;
reckless – leichtsinnig

you into *every* apartment and *every* house, understood?"

Isy and Amanda nodded obediently and felt uncomfortably hot in their wigs. As soon as they were outside with Alfredo, they heaved a sigh of relief. It was a good job that Mr Rimpau was in a hurry to get to the airport. If he had called their parents, they would have been grounded for the rest of the holidays, which didn't bear thinking about!

"Let's go to Max's place," said Isy weakly, still recovering from their ordeal. They made their way to the untidiest apartment in Berlin to administer Leila's daily dose of vitamins and fresh lettuce. After that, they emptied Mrs Ober-Lippe's mailbox, fed the canaries in Neukölln, watered the plants in Britz, and stopped off in Karlshorst to check on Gottfried. Isy and Amanda suspected that Mrs Knosalla had won her precious pet in another competition – Japanese goldfish were expensive.

"The travelling is the worst part," groaned Amanda while they waited for the bus to take them to Mrs von Leinungen's cats in Charlottenburg. "The rest of the job is quite fun."

Isy agreed with her. It was exciting to unlock the doors and know that someone was relying on them to take care of their beloved pets and plants. And when they locked the doors behind them, they knew that the inhabitants of the apartments were fed, watered and happy. In fact, Isy and Amanda took special care to tickle, stroke and comfort them. Amanda saw herself as a plant-whisperer and spoke lovingly to the greenery, including the ivy.

But most of their time was spent journeying back and forth through Berlin. And from tomorrow they would be adding three more duties to the list: the tomcat from Wilmersdorf, the conservatory in Weissensee, and Wolfram B. Braun's grandma in Berlin-Mitte.

Isy decided that they would have to split up. They would never get through all the apartments unless they divided the list between them. She resolved not to say anything until they were in Charlottenburg. It was obvious that Amanda wouldn't take to the idea.

"Are you crazy?" screeched Amanda as they made their way to Otti and Lotti's. "Didn't you hear what Mr Rimpau told us?"

"You shouldn't pay attention to him! He always imagines the worst!'

Darkness had descended over Berlin, but Charlottenburg's shop windows and streetlights were **radiantly** bright. It was a shame that they didn't have time to admire the stylish merchandise and allow themselves to dream a little. Otti and Lotti's stomachs would be rumbling by now.

"What have you decided to cook for them?"

"Chinese stir-fry," muttered Amanda. It sounded as though she was still sulking.

"Mmm, lovely!" Isy stopped under a streetlight and peered into the bag of keys. She found the key to Mrs von Leinungen's apartment, pushed open the heavy door to the apartment block, and tied Al-

---

radiant – strahlend

fredo to the magnificently carved **banisters**. It didn't seem wise to introduce him to the cats. Isy was halfway up the staircase when she heard her friend muttering under her breath.

"What did you say, Amanda?"

"Nothing."

"Come on, Amanda, I heard you."

"I said I won't do it. I'm not going into strangers' houses on my own."

"Don't be such a **wet blanket**!" Isy fumbled nervously with Mrs von Leinungen's lock. The door wouldn't open. "You shouldn't let people frighten you like that. What's the worst that could happen?" The door opened suddenly and Isy turned on the lights.

Amanda pointed to the hallway in horror. Her face was deathly pale.

Isy stared at the devastation, too shocked to move. Something awful had happened! Mrs von Leinungen's possessions were scattered across the floor.

Sheets, pillowcases, tablecloths and towels were strewn throughout the hallway. The carved doors of the wooden cabinet were open, and the drawers had been turned out.

Amanda placed a clammy hand on Isy's shoulder. "Let's get out of here," she whispered.

"What about the cats?" hissed Isy. Heart racing, she crept towards the lounge.

---

banister – Treppengeländer;
wet blanket – Spielverderber

"We'd better call the police!"

"Not on your life!" Isy reached for the door. It was **ajar**. Slowly, she pushed it open and peered into the darkness, not knowing what she might find. She took a deep breath, turned on the lights and heaved a sigh of relief. The room looked the same as always. Even the antique armchair was exactly where Mrs von Leinungen had left it.

"All clear," she told her friend who was standing motionless in the hall. "I'll check the other rooms."

Under normal circumstances, Isy would never venture into a client's bedroom, but Mrs von Leinungen would surely understand. She scanned the room and saw a bed and a wooden chest of drawers. Nothing had been touched, or at least there was no sign that anyone had been in there. The finely woven blue **throw** was spread neatly over the bed, and every single one of the drawers in the antique dresser was tightly closed. Mrs von Leinungen didn't seem to have a wardrobe.

Relieved, she went back into the hall where Amanda was comforting Otti and Lotti.

Purring contentedly, the cats pressed themselves against her curly blonde wig.

"They were hiding," said Amanda in distress. "I hate to think what they've been through."

Isy gave them both a stroke. "It looks as though the intruder only **rifled** through the hall."

---

ajar – einen Spalt offen;
throw – Überdecke;
to rifle – plündern

"Good," said Amanda. "Now can we call the police?"

"Why not call Detective Rose in person? I'm sure he'll be delighted to arrest the two suspects."

Amanda straightened up and looked at her blankly. "Two suspects?"

"Two angels under the age of eighteen, both wearing a disguise and working for an agency that doesn't exist. Oh, and carrying a bunch of keys to other people's houses."

"But we've got witnesses!"

"Witnesses? They're all on holiday!"

"The police will know we're telling the truth. Detective Rose will believe us – he knows us from school!"

"Oh sure, he'll believe us; it's just a question of when. They'll keep us in **custody** until they've worked out the truth." Isy saw Amanda's eyes widen in horror at the prospect of jail. "Afterwards, they'll call our parents and we'll never be allowed to work again."

Long moments of silence passed. A clock was ticking loudly in one of the rooms. Suddenly the cats meowed, and Amanda remembered her duty. With a sigh, she pulled a plastic container from her rucksack. "I cooked it earlier. It just needs heating up." She scanned the hallway nervously and disappeared into the kitchen.

"You're a star," called Isy after her. "I'll take care of the litter tray."

---

custody – Gewahrsam

While she was emptying the litter tray and filling it with a fresh layer of straw, her mind was working at double-speed. Mrs von Leinungen had told them that she suspected someone had been into her apartment and moved her chair. She had even mentioned that an anonymous caller kept phoning to check on her movements. Isy was ashamed to admit that she hadn't believed her.

"Do you know what's strange, Amanda?" called Isy, following the **tantalizing** smell from the stove. "The apartment hadn't been broken into! The intruder must have let himself in with a key. The locks will have to be changed, but the whole thing is a bit of a mystery. Why didn't he search the other rooms?"

Amanda licked the **ladle**. "Maybe whatever he was looking for was in the hall."

The answer didn't satisfy Isy. "OK, let's assume he found it. Why didn't he clear away the evidence?"

"In that case, perhaps he didn't find it," replied Amanda, scooping the stir-fry into Otti and Lotti's bowls. The cats meowed excitedly, but Amanda scarcely noticed. Isy's questions were making her nervous.

"Exactly! That's the obvious conclusion, but surely he would have searched the rest of the apartment ... In my opinion, there's only one explanation." Isy paused for a moment, allowing the

---

tantalizing – *(hier)* verlockend;
ladle – Schöpfkelle

suspense to grow. "He must have been interrupted!"

"What?" Amanda's face paled to the colour of her beloved mozzarella cheese. "You're not suggesting that … I mean, you don't really think we … Are you saying he was here when we arrived?"

"Think about it! The door was **jammed** when I tried to open it. It felt like someone was pushing it from the other side!"

They stared at each other in silence, hardly daring to breathe.

It was then that Isy remembered her rash words to Mr Rimpau: 'It's perfectly safe. The owners will be on holiday, their flats will be empty, and it won't be the least bit dangerous – unless we get pricked by a cactus!'

If only she hadn't said anything! It was **anything but** safe!

"Are you thinking what I'm thinking?" she asked, lowering her voice to a whisper. Instead of replying, Amanda clapped a hand to her mouth.

Just then they heard a noise in the hallway. It sounded like footsteps. Then the front door slammed shut. Alfredo was barking excitedly in the stairwell.

"Stop!" shouted Isy. "Stop right there!" Without thinking she charged down the hallway, but Amanda grabbed her and refused to let go.

"Don't leave me alone!" she whimpered. Merci-

---

to jam – verklemmen;
anything but – alles andere als

fully, her panic attack was extremely brief: at that moment she **fainted**.

"Pull yourself together," said Isy when Amanda finally woke up from her faint. The cats had finished their stir-fry, and Alfredo had stopped barking. She stroked her friend's cheek. "I think we've found ourselves a new case!"

— 9 —

"**New twist** in the saga of missing schoolgirl Josepha Boskov," announced the headlines the following day.

The news was all over the front page of Mrs Ober-Lippe's daily newspaper. Isy took it out of the mailbox, grabbing hold of a telephone bill at the same time. The report stated that Josepha's mother had come into a large inheritance at the start of the summer. It was a possible motive for a kidnapping. Someone might be holding Josepha for ransom.

Isy decided that the news bode well for Josepha. It was about time that the police came up with a motive. So far the search had been based on guesswork and speculation, but if Josepha was being held for ransom, she was almost certainly alive. Comforted by the thought, Isy slipped the **leash** around Alfredo's neck and left Mrs Ober-Lippe's apartment. Her next stop was Charlottenburg, where

---

to faint – ohnmächtig werden;
leash – Hundeleine

she would hopefully arrive in Kant Street at the same time as Amanda. Last night, she had persuaded her friend to deliver the bread and milk to Wolfram B. Braun's grandmother on her own. It meant that Amanda, who loved her sleep, was forced to leave her cosy bed at seven in the morning – but it was either that or enter a stranger's apartment on her own. The mere idea of it terrified Amanda, especially after what had happened the previous day. Isy knew that her friend was already a nervous wreck. Poor Bumblebee!

Amanda looked pale and nervous when she appeared out of the shadows near the entrance to Mrs von Leinungen's apartment block. She hurried towards Isy.

"This time we'll take Alfredo with us, OK?" she said anxiously. The schnauzer leapt up at her and licked her. "I'm not going inside without him!"

Isy nodded. "Don't worry, the cats didn't seem to mind too much when the three of us searched the apartment last night."

If truth be told, only two of them had searched the apartment. Isy and Alfredo had scoured every inch of the premises and discovered a **dressing room** where the intruder had waited for an opportunity to escape. In the meantime, the trembling Amanda had armed herself with a silver **carving fork** and taken up position behind the kitchen table.

---

dressing room – Kleiderkammer;
carving fork – Tranchiergabel

They were halfway up the stairs when a well-dressed elderly couple passed them in the opposite direction. They looked at them suspiciously. Isy and Amanda were used to that by now: their angel outfits tended to cause a stir.

"Any problems with granny's shopping?" enquired Isy.

Amanda shook her head. She had delivered the bag punctually to apartment 1101. "I hope no one steals it!"

"It's not our fault if they do. Mr Braun specifically asked us not to ring the doorbell." Isy pushed the key **tentatively** into the lock. This time the door opened effortlessly.

Amanda grabbed her friend's hand. "Let Alfredo go first!"

For all his friendly nature, the schnauzer could be relied on to protect them. He was a decently sized dog, and his **innate** toughness and fearlessness would come in handy if they were attacked. Luckily, his fighting spirit wasn't put to the test.

Amanda looked visibly relieved and strode into the kitchen to warm up Otti and Lotti's spring rolls. Isy turned her attention to the litter tray, then set about tidying the hall. She had no idea where Mrs von Leinungen kept her things, but it didn't really matter. Her goal was simply to stow everything into the cabinet so that the hall didn't look like a bombsite. When she was finished, she went into

---

tentative – unsicher, versuchend;
innate – angeboren

the lounge and fetched the piece of paper with the contact details for the bridge club from the old lady's bureau.

They had decided to break the news about the intruder as gently as possible. Mrs von Leinungen might have a weak heart, and Isy wanted to reassure her that everything was under control. She dialled the number and waited for someone to pick up. At last she heard a female voice: "Brinkenbühl Mill! Reverend Green's office!"

"Good morning. Is that the bridge club?" asked Isy.

"Sorry, wrong number," replied the voice, and rang off.

Isy checked the piece of paper again. She must have made a mistake. Patiently, she dialled the number and heard the same voice. This time the woman sounded cross: "Didn't I make myself clear? This isn't the bridge club!" Isy heard a click: the woman had hung up without another word. She stared at the telephone **incredulously**. Had Mrs von Leinungen given them the wrong number? Amanda was never going to believe it …

"I can't believe it," said Amanda, who was cooking in a haze of oily smoke under the watchful gaze of Otti, Lotti and Alfredo. "What do you mean, the wrong number?"

Isy was about to answer when someone rang the doorbell. Alfredo started barking.

---

incredulous – ungläubig

Amanda disappeared behind the kitchen table like a shot. "Don't open it!"

"Stop panicking," said Isy, trying not to grin. "It's only Gummy Bear."

She followed the excited Alfredo into the hallway and opened the door.

Gummy Bear looked at her suspiciously. "Why are you dressed like that?"

"No reason. It's just a fancy-dress costume. Come in!"

Gummy Bear picked up his father's toolbox and stepped into the hall. He looked around warily. "Are you sure your aunt lives here? I didn't think your family was **posh**."

"We're not posh! I mean, my aunt's posh, but we're not …" To cover her embarrassment, she quickly showed Gummy Bear the old lock and fetched the new one for him to inspect. Her father had bought it at a DIY store ages ago, and it had been lying in a cupboard ever since. "Do you think you can do it?"

"Give me a moment," growled Gummy Bear, opening the toolbox. He glanced at Alfredo. "Don't I know him?"

"Of course you know him! It's Alfredo, Mr Rimpau's dog!" Amanda stuck her blonde polyester wig around the kitchen door and peered into the hall. "You remember Mr Rimpau, don't you? We met him last autumn at the field centre in Altgrünheide."

---

posh – vornehm

Hagen Golz, nicknamed Gummy Bear because of his passion for jelly sweets, had no trouble recalling Mr Rimpau. In particular, he remembered how Isy and Amanda had seen him climbing a ladder one night and mistaken him for a thief. They had used his own burglar deterrent against him, and he had been lucky to escape with his life. In Gummy Bear's opinion, Isy and Amanda were seriously dangerous. They weren't calamity queens; they were **hell raisers**!

Gummy Bear gazed at the lock and decided that something was wrong. Isy and her **roly-poly** friend from Nuremberg were up to their usual tricks. Why else would they be dressed up like angels in a posh apartment with Mr Rimpau's dog? And why else would they want him to replace a lock that wasn't even broken?

He had smelt a rat as soon as Isy had phoned for his help. The fact was, Isolde Schütze and Amanda Bornstein had a charming habit of relying on him to extract them from their disasters. They were always stumbling upon thieves, criminals and other wrongdoers. He remembered the case of the missing mail last autumn in Altgrünheide, then the stolen falcon's eggs this spring at the zoo. His instincts told him that they were planning something similar again. He wondered whether they had decided to look for Josepha on their own. After all, Mrs Boskov had inherited half a million euros

---

hell raiser – Höllengeist;
roly-poly – mollig

and was bound to offer a reward. Gummy Bear decided to keep an eye on the girls while he played the role of the obedient **handyman**. Whistling **jauntily**, he got down to work.

Meanwhile, Isy and Amanda were conferring in the kitchen. Had Mrs von Leinungen given them the wrong number on purpose?

"It must have been a mistake," ruled Isy. She watched as Amanda **rummaged** through the drawers in search of an implement for turning the rolls in the pan.

"The spring rolls smell fantastic," Isy told her. "Did you make them yourself?"

"No, IGLO made them for me. I pinched them from the freezer."

Amanda took a spatula from the drawer and turned the Chinese **treats**. The animals' eyes tracked her every movement.

"Maybe I should call the operator and ask for the number of the bridge club," suggested Isy. "The address is in Brinkenbühl."

She disappeared into the lounge and made herself comfortable in Mrs von Leinungen's armchair while she waited for an answer. A look of **bewilderment** crossed her face, and she made her way back to the kitchen.

---

handyman – Heimwerker;
jaunty – munter;
to rummage – herumkramen;
treat – Leckerbissen;
bewilderment – Verwirrung

"There isn't a bridge club in Brinkenbühl," she told her friend. "It hasn't got a bridge club, only an old mill."

"Says who?"

"The regional council. The operator put me through to them."

Amanda seemed puzzled. She **shovelled** the spring rolls out of the pan and left them to cool on a plate. "But if Mrs von Leinungen isn't in Brinkenbühl, where on earth is she?"

"Who knows?" sighed Isy. Mrs von Leinungen was beginning to get on her nerves. It wasn't their fault that someone had broken into her apartment. She and Amanda were supposed to be looking after Otti and Lotti, not playing detective. No one was going to pay them for their time!

She was in the middle of watering the thirsty myrtle plant when Gummy Bear stuck his head around the door. "Aren't you going to offer me a Coke or something?" he enquired. "You should probably mop up the blood in the bathroom. It looks like a horror film in there!"

"Blood?" echoed Isy and Amanda, aghast.

Gummy Bear led the way into the bathroom and pointed behind the washstand to a long trail of dried blood. "Who've you been **slaughtering**? You might look angelic but you can't fool me!"

"Yuck!" gasped Amanda. "I think I'm going to be sick!"

---

to shovel – schaufeln;
to slaughter – schlachten

Isy was staring pale-faced at the **gory** streak of blood. Why hadn't they noticed it before? Perhaps it was the excitement, or maybe the bad light. But none of that was important. What had happened in the bathroom? Who had lost all that blood? Did it come from the intruder or from Mrs von Leinungen?

Had Mrs von Leinungen hurt herself? Had someone hurt Mrs von Leinungen? Had Mrs von Leinungen been *abducted*?

– 10 –

The low pressure system was called Hertha. It left Scandinavia overnight and brought heavy storms to northern Germany. In the course of the morning, it reached Berlin, whose inhabitants were struck down with headaches, fatigue and general exhaustion. The forecaster had been right.

Isy was feeling the pressure as well, but it was nothing to do with Hertha. She was **racking her brains**, trying to figure out a way of persuading Amanda to hop on a bus with her to Brinkenbühl. Meanwhile, Amanda was **luxuriating** in a pale green rattan chair in Britz.

It seemed to Isy that Mrs von Leinungen must have been abducted and that she and Amanda

---

gory – grausig;
to rack one's brains – sich den Kopf zerbrechen;
to luxuriate – es sich gut gehen lassen

would have to take action. They couldn't sit back and leave the old lady to her fate.

"Watch what you're doing, Isy," said Amanda, pointing to a plant with dark green leaves. "This one needs warm water, not cold." She was referring to the instructions on an information chart that the owners had left for them. The calathea was **apparently** a sensitive plant that would curl up its beautiful velvety leaves if treated anything less than kindly.

Isy sprayed the majestic palms and plucked the dead leaves from the **weeping figs**. She peered into the front garden and watched a fat, grey cat **skulking** through the grass. Isy felt like telling it not to waste its time; the birds would all be sheltering in the trees. In weather like this, only the leaves dared to fly across the lawn, skimming over the grass, rustling against the windows, and spiralling over the glass roof. There was a quiet beauty to the suburban garden in spite of the storm. Isy tried to imagine how stunning it would look in the summertime.

"Did you see the detective show last night?" she asked Amanda.

"I hate detective shows," her friend said vehemently. She buried her head in the glossy magazine that she had found on the sofa in the lounge. "You should know that by now!"

---

apparent – anscheinend;
weeping fig – Birkenfeige;
to skulk – umherschleichen

"I do," said Isy soothingly, "but it was about a... Well, it was about someone who left their relatives a fortune in their will. It got me thinking. What if the intruder was burgling Mrs von Leinungen's apartment in order to steal her will? In detective films, old people are always getting killed or burgled because they're rich."

"Whatever," mumbled Amanda. Suddenly she sat up straight. "Poor Lady Di! It says here Charles had lots of other **mistresses**!"

"For pity's sake, Amanda! He's welcome to have hundreds of lovers, one for every day of the year. You know I'm not interested in your trashy gossip magazines."

"And I'm not interested in your boring old will."

"What do you mean, my will? Mrs von Leinungen's life is at stake! Until we know for sure that it wasn't her blood streaked all over the bathroom, we'll have to assume she's been abducted."

"Abducted? You've got to be joking! Besides, how are we supposed to find out if it was her blood? Gummy Bear mopped it up."

She was right. What would the forensic experts say when they realized that Hagen Golz had eliminated every last trace of the evidence? It wasn't his fault, though. He had taken pity on Isy and Amanda because they looked so pale and shocked.

"But we need to find out where it came from!"

"I'd be more interested if you could tell me where the toilet is," said Amanda, sighing as she

---

mistress Mätresse

levered herself out of the fancy green chair. She glanced at the three watches on her wrist. "I mustn't be late today." Her face darkened. "I've got toothache. And anyway, it's my cookery class tonight. I need to save some energy for that."

Disappointed, Isy checked their list of duties. It was typical of Amanda to care more about her stupid pasta than Mrs von Leinungen's safety.

"OK, so we've nearly finished here. Next we've got Fred in Neukölln and Wolodja in Wilmersdorf. And then we can go to my place."

"To your place? What for?"

"There's something I want to talk about."

For a split-second Amanda looked interested, then she scowled. "I know what you're up to, Isolde. You think you can talk me into going to Brinkenbühl and looking for the bridge club. I'm telling you now, I won't do it."

"I won't do it," she said again after they had completed their duties, changed their clothes and **munched** their way through a mountain of sandwiches. "I've had enough of your overactive imagination. You're always on the lookout for an adventure."

Isy smiled grimly. "OK, Amanda, I'll call in at the police station and tell them what's happened. I won't be held responsible if something awful happens to the poor lady."

---

to lever – hebeln;
to munch – schmatzend kauen

"Isy, you can't! They'll tell our parents!"

"It's your choice," said Isy pitilessly, sharing the last corner of her sandwich with Alfredo.

"That's blackmail!" hissed Amanda.

At that moment the telephone rang in the hallway. They stared at each other in surprise.

"I thought you said it wasn't working?" said Amanda accusingly.

"It wasn't! My dad must have fixed it." She went into the hall and picked up the receiver.

"*Making Holidays Happen!* How can I help?" she said mechanically. Suddenly Amanda appeared beside her and whispered in her ear: "Tell them that we're too busy, or else!"

Amanda marched back into the kitchen and sat down at the table. She was furious at Isy for being so **mean**. Friends weren't supposed to blackmail each other!

"Friends aren't supposed to blackmail each other!" she sobbed when Isy put down the phone. "I didn't think you could be so mean!"

"What else am I supposed to do? Someone needs to rescue Mrs von Leinungen!"

"But not us!"

"Then who?" demanded Isy. Amanda blew her nose.

"Aren't you going to ask who called?"

"Who?"

Isy smiled mysteriously and kept quiet.

---

mean – gemein

"Go on, then, tell me! It wasn't someone famous was it?"

Isy gave a little nod, and Amanda almost jumped out of her seat. "Don't tell me you said ..."

Isy shook her head.

"Thank goodness for that! We're too busy to take on any more clients, regardless of how famous they are!" She looked out of the window and watched the storm caused by Hertha. Fat droplets rolled down the glass. "So who was it?"

"Have a guess!"

"Not the Chancellor?"

Isy grinned. "Well, no, not exactly. And it wasn't Prince William either."

Amanda bit her lip. "OK, just tell me!"

"I can't."

"Pretty, pretty please!"

"All right, it was your hero, Pioschleck. He said he's been trying to reach us for days."

"What?" shrieked Amanda, getting up quickly and almost overturning the table. "Pio? And you turned him away? I can't believe it!!"

She **slumped** down **forlornly**. Isy had never seen her look so miserable.

"Cheer up, Amanda!" she said, patting her arm affectionately. "Of course I didn't turn him away! I couldn't be so cruel!"

---

to slump – hinplumpsen;
forlorn – unglücklich, hoffnungslos

— 11 —

The constant drone of the bus was only slightly less **tedious** than the monotony of the scenery.

For thirty minutes the view had consisted entirely of dripping wet pine trees and sandy Brandenburg soil. Every now and then they spotted fields that had recently been harvested, tall windmills with sharp metal blades, and houses whose pale red roofs sat low over their stony faces.

Dusk was draping its dark veil across the countryside.

Isy and Amanda were sitting at the front of the bus behind the driver. Amanda's head was propped on Isy's shoulders and she was fast asleep. It had been a tough day so far, but Isy was in high spirits. Professor Pioschleck's phone call had put Amanda in such a good mood that she had agreed to accompany her friend to Brinkenbühl in spite of her reservations. Isy could feel the excitement growing with every kilometre. Would they find the right address? Would Mrs von Leinungen be there?

Even if there was no sign of the old lady, the mill would surely give them some answers. Why else would Mrs von Leinungen have left them the address? Isy hoped that all would be revealed.

From time to time the bus braked gently to let one or other of the passengers get on or off. Most of them stared at Isy and Amanda in surprise. Out here in the countryside, their costumes attracted

---

tedious – langwierig

more attention than in the city. At last the driver shouted "Brinkenbühl!" and Isy gave Amanda a little shake.

"Where am I?" she murmured, looking sleepily at Isy.

"Hurry up!" ordered Isy, dragging her towards the door. "We're in Brinkenbühl!"

"Brinken-what?" said Amanda, stepping off the bus.

She felt the cold, **dank** air on her face, and woke up **with a start**. She wasn't wandering through a shimmering desert in Egypt. As far as she could tell, she was in a village in Brandenburg. A single bumpy road ran straight through the middle.

Isy was surveying her surroundings, too. "This is going to be child's play, Amanda! The whole village won't take more than ten minutes to explore. Hopefully we'll be able to ask for directions."

Unfortunately there was no one in sight. A couple of cars sped past, and a dog barked excitedly in a garden, but that was all. At last an elderly woman loomed out of the darkness on a **rickety** old bicycle. She was weighed down with shopping bags.

"Hello there," called Isy. "We're looking for the bridge club!"

The woman stared at her in bewilderment, then put on a burst of speed.

Isy was about to shout after her indignantly, but Amanda burst out laughing.

---

dank – unangenehm feucht;
with a start – mit einem Ruck; rickety – klapprig

"I don't blame her! She's probably never seen a holiday angel. I bet we scared her to death!"

"I should have thought of that," said Isy crossly. She would have to remember in future that their outfits were liable to cause alarm. "The passengers in the bus were staring at us, too."

They **trudged** determinedly through the village, hoping to find a shop where they would be able to ask for help. Oddly enough, they weren't having much success. Isy could only assume that the shops were clustered around a marketplace out of sight of the road.

"There's got to be a bakery somewhere in this godforsaken village," moaned Amanda.

"Unless the villagers make do with food for the soul!" said Isy, pulling her friend into a tiny bookshop. A bell rang as they walked through the door and stepped into the warmth. The woman at the counter took off her reading glasses and looked at them in astonishment. "Christmas angels at this time of year?"

"We're holiday angels, actually," Isy corrected her. She had taken an instant liking to the woman. In fact, she liked the whole shop. Isy always felt at home in bookshops. It was a shame they didn't have time to look around.

"We're looking for a mill," explained Amanda, cleaning her plastic glasses on her sleeve. "It's the venue for the bridge club."

"The bridge club?" said the woman, puzzled.

---

to trudge – mühsam laufen

"I've never heard of a bridge club – but no one really knows what goes on inside the mill."

"Could you tell us how to get there?" asked Isy.

"I can drop you off at the front door, if you like. It's on my way home, and my daughter-in-law will be here in a moment to start her shift."

"That would be brilliant!" said Amanda gratefully. Ten minutes later they were on their way to Brinkenbühl mill in an old Ford with squeaking suspension. Isy was tempted to interrogate the woman about the mill, but she decided it was too risky. Luckily the bookseller introduced the topic herself.

"Are you performing at the mill?" she asked, turning onto a bumpy road that was bordered by trees. Isy watched anxiously as the mist crept along the ground. That was all they needed!

"Er, no. We're just... We're visiting my aunt!" she said. It didn't feel right to lie to someone who was doing them a favour. "She's on holiday here."

"The old folks seem to love the mill," observed the woman, nodding in satisfaction. "Young people sometimes stay there, too. Years ago it was a **run-down** place – almost a ruin, you could say. After **reunification** a rich businessman turned it into a fancy mansion. I've never been inside. Apparently, the prices are **extortionate**." She turned off the road and stopped in front of a large lawn. "Of

---

run-down – heruntergekommen, verfallen;
reunification – Wiedervereinigung;
extortionate – halsabschneiderisch

course, there are all kinds of rumours. People say that odd things go on in there, but it's probably just talk." She pointed to an imposing timber building. A wild vine had spread its **tendrils** over the walls. "This is it: Brinkenbühl mill."

Amanda was the first to squeeze out of the car. "Cool building!" she said admiringly. "But where are the **sails**?"

The woman chuckled. "Brinkenbühl mill was a watermill, not a windmill!"

She shook hands with Isy and Amanda, and the two friends thanked her profusely. Then the old Ford spluttered away into the shifting veil of mist and dusk.

Isy realized with **trepidation** that she and Amanda were on their own. The garden seemed unnervingly quiet. It was the perfect place for an abduction or a kidnapping. Her thoughts turned to Alfredo, who was being looked after by Gummy Bear. Maybe they should have brought him with them?

Amanda seemed to be thinking the same. She gripped Isy's hand nervously.

"Did you hear what she said? Odd things happen at the mill! If only Alfredo were here!"

"That's exactly what I was thinking! But Alfredo would bark like mad and give us away. We'd better get it over with. In half an hour we won't be able to see a thing."

---

tendril – Wickelranke;
sail – *(hier)* Flügel; trepidation – Ängstlichkeit

Isy and Amanda hurried across the **cobbled** forecourt and walked a circuit of the building in search of an open window. They found one in the conservatory. The room was deserted.

Amanda pressed her back against the wall. "How do you play bridge?"

Isy shrugged. "No idea! I thought you might know, actually." She paused for a moment. "Trust me, Amanda: this isn't a bridge club! The woman from the bookshop said that old people come here – old people with money. They're exactly the sort who get **bumped off**!"

She grabbed the window ledge, hauled herself up, and jumped into the conservatory. In the dim light she could make out a green armchair, a sideboard, and a chair with purple upholstery. A tall lamp with a silk lampshade stood next to a wooden cabinet with a mirror that Isy recognized. She tried to remember where she had seen it, then gave up and helped Amanda through the window. They **huddled together** for a moment and listened to the cheerful hum of conversation. Luckily, the voices seemed to be coming from a long way away.

"I'll check the corridor," whispered Isy. Suddenly Amanda gave a **muffled** shriek and pointed to something on the sideboard. Isy spotted it, too. A

---

cobbled – mit Kopfsteinpflaster bedeckt;
to bump s.o. off (slang) – jmdn. umbringen;
to huddle together – sich zusammenkauern;
muffled – gedämpft

silver pistol was lying on the elegant cherrywood surface. It glinted coldly in the shadowy light.

"Don't panic!" said Isy sternly. "It's not real!"

"Not real? How do you know?"

"I can see it's not real!"

"Then why is it here?"

"To scare people off. To frighten intruders – like you and me!"

"You're making it up!" hissed Amanda.

She was right. Isy had no idea why the pistol was there, but she was prepared to lie if it stopped Amanda panicking.

They **tiptoed** to the door and opened it gradually until they could see into the rest of the mansion. Isy looked at the long marble corridor. It was lined with doors and passageways on both sides. The noise was coming from the other end: chattering voices, clinking glasses and laughter. Isy felt sorry for the unsuspecting guests. The gangsters were probably filling their glasses and charming them with smiles. It was lucky that Isy knew a thing or two about the reality of life. Thank goodness she had read all those crime novels! The conservatory led into the hallway, and a red-carpeted staircase ascended to the upper floors. Isy guessed that the bedrooms were upstairs. To her intense relief, there was still no sign of anyone.

"Have you turned off your mobile?" she asked Amanda, who nodded meekly. Signalling for her to follow, Isy crept out of the room.

---

to tiptoe – auf Zehenspitzen laufen

— 12 —

The mansion was huge – big enough to get lost in – and everything about it was impeccably stylish. Amanda stopped trembling for a moment and looked around with starry eyes. The furnishings were divine!

"What are we going to say if they catch us?" she asked as they hurried down the long white marble corridor.

"We won't say anything! We'll run!"

Isy pushed open a door and stared into the dining room. The enormous table was made of walnut and in the middle were three candles in a brass candlestick. The dining chairs were covered in russet-coloured velvet. To the left of the door was a green sofa, and to the right was a cabinet filled with exquisite china. The table was laid for dinner.

Isy closed the door hurriedly, hoping that Amanda hadn't spotted the steel **dagger** glinting on the antique sideboard. Mrs von Leinungen's abductors were armed to the teeth!

"This way," she hissed, making a beeline for the next room which she guessed was the kitchen. Footsteps hurried towards them. Isy grabbed her friend's hand and pulled her behind the stairs.

They were just **in the nick of time**.

A slim blonde woman in a green woollen cape strode past their hiding place in the direction of the

---

dagger – Dolch;
in the nick of time – gerade noch rechtzeitig

hall. Isy could scarcely believe her eyes. "Did you make an appointment for your toothache?" she asked Amanda.

"No, I ... What do you mean, Isy?"

"That was our dentist, stupid!"

Amanda's jaw fell open. "Dr Schley? Don't be **ridiculous**!" she said disapprovingly. How heartless of Isy to **tease** her when there were killers in the house! Then it dawned on her that maybe it wasn't a joke. She knew for a fact that Dr Schley's practice was closed. The dentist was away for a week, and Marianne, the kind-hearted nurse who took care of her terrified patients, was on holiday as well.

"Do you think she's in danger?"

"She might be ... Or maybe she's part of the danger! She's got tons of anaesthetics at her disposal!"

Before Amanda could start a discussion, Isy grabbed her arm and dragged her down the corridor in the opposite direction. They crossed the hall quickly.

"They're still in the lounge," she whispered. "Let's keep looking." She pulled her friend towards three doors made of dark wood. Then she thought about what she had said: *the lounge*. How could she possibly know whether the room at the end of the corridor was a lounge or not?

She had a funny feeling that the next room would turn out to be the library. Frozen with shock,

---

ridiculous – lächerlich;
to tease – necken

she stared at the desk, the Tiffany lamp, the old silver candlestick, and the floor-to-ceiling shelves that were stacked with rows of books. How had she known it would look like this?

If the next room turned out to be the billiard room, it was proof that she had been here before. But she had never visited Brinkenbühl in her life.

They **darted** down the corridor and opened the door. It was a billiard room.

The green baize table stood next to the window. The carpet was olive green and the bar was positioned to the right of the door. There was a rope lying ominously on the counter. Isy had seen it all before.

"I think I'm going mad," she told Amanda. "It looks so familiar."

"I know what you mean," her friend stammered. "Do you think it was the set of a detective series?"

A detective series? It was a plausible explanation, but Isy didn't have time to consider the matter further. Finding Mrs von Leinungen was her priority, and everything else would have to wait.

"There's no one here," she whispered. "Let's take a look upstairs."

They crept across the hall and reached the bottom of the staircase. Suddenly a man in a green suit leaned over the banisters and peered down at them. "Stop! Where do you think you're going? Who gave you permission to come in?"

They turned and ran **pell-mell** towards the near-

---

to dart – huschen; pell-mell – holterdiepolter

est room. It was dark inside except for the glow from the flickering hearth. Isy pulled Amanda into a shadowy corner. They stopped in front of a purple leather armchair and a corner cabinet filled with books.

"They'll find us!" wailed Amanda. "We're done for!"

"Don't be defeatist," hissed Isy. "There's light at the end of the tunnel – and not just metaphorically! Surely you recognize the fireplace? This is the study! There should be a secret passageway right here!" She ran her hand over the wooden panelling by the window. Voices sounded from the corridor.

"Two angels!" a man was saying impatiently. "They were here a second ago. They can't have disappeared!"

"Angels?" said a woman disbelievingly. "Reverend Green, are you sure?"

"Of course I'm sure! I'm going to tell Colonel Mustard. We'll have to search the park and the fitness centre, pool, sauna and solarium. You'd better start with the rooms down here. Check the study first!"

"Hurry up, they're coming," **whimpered** Amanda.

"I'm trying," Isy told her. She was in a cold sweat. "I can't find the right spot!"

Just then the wooden panelling slid away beneath her fumbling fingers. Silently, the secret

---

to whimper – winseln

door came open to reveal a staircase leading underground.

Isy **yanked** her friend into the passageway. A second later, the light flicked on and someone peered into the room.

"I can't see any angels," a woman announced dryly.

Her companion giggled. "Reverend Green must have been overdoing it with the pre-dinner drinks!"

The door to the study closed.

Isy was overcome with relief. "Blimey, that was close!"

"But … but how did you know about the secret passageway?" asked a sobbing Amanda.

Poor Bumblebee. It was all too much.

"I don't know," admitted Isy, still feeling slightly shaky. She sat down next to Amanda on the steps, then jumped up in panic. "Come on, Amanda, we've got to get out of here!"

They rushed down the stairs and started down a dimly lit underground passageway. At last they came to a solid oak door with metal **hasps**.

"Maybe it opens into the garden," said Amanda hopefully. "We might catch the last bus home. I'm starving!"

"I reckon it's the kitchen, not the garden," replied Isy, giving the heavy door a push. It seemed to be jammed, so she rattled the handle. She didn't

---

to yank – hastig zerren;
hasp – Eisenbeschlag

expect it to open, but it did. She and Amanda tumbled into the room.

Dazzled by the sudden light, they peered at the spacious kitchen and the chequered floor. The housekeeper had just disappeared down the corridor with a tray of food. Amanda leapt forward and grabbed a **chicken drumstick** from the sideboard. Mouth-watering goodies were piled high on dinner plates. Isy stared at the floor. The tiles looked oddly familiar. She was struck by a sudden realization. At last it all made sense.

"Amanda!" she gasped. "I've worked out how I knew about the tunnel! Do you know why everything looks so familiar? It isn't because of a detective series! It's because of Cluedo!"

– 13 –

There was no doubt about it: they were in the Cluedo mansion.

The building had exactly the same layout as the famous board game. Each of the rooms had been furnished according to Cluedo's specifications, and Isy was feverishly trying to work out why. Her thoughts were interrupted by the return of the housekeeper. She and Amanda **scurried** behind the fridge.

They peered out as a woman in a white apron

---

chicken drumstick – Hühnerschlegel;
to scurry – huschen

placed a plate of succulent vegetables on her tray. She shuffled round and revealed her face to the hidden observers. Isy almost jumped for joy.

"Watch out for falling china!" she whispered to Amanda. Without warning, she stepped out from behind the fridge and said softly, "Good evening Mrs von Leinungen!"

There was an almighty crash as the tray crashed to the floor, then the old lady composed herself. "Good evening, holiday angels! What are you doing here?"

Isy and Amanda rushed over and bombarded her with questions. "How are you? Are you really OK? How did they abduct you? Are you being held against your will?"

"Against my will? Good heavens, no!" replied Mrs von Leinungen. "Whatever gave you that idea?"

"So no one's forcing you to stay?" persisted Isy.

Gudrun von Leinungen shook her head, puzzled.

"Then why did you lie to us about the bridge club?"

"Oh!" A pink **flush** spread over Mrs von Leinungen's cheeks. "I was too embarrassed to tell you the truth. I'm a bit old to belong to a Cluedo club. People of my age are supposed to play bridge." She gave a guilty smile. "The fact is, everyone here is crazy about Cluedo."

"You mean, the murder weapons aren't real?" asked Isy.

---

flush – Erröten

"Of course they're not real! We're Cluedo players, not killers!"

Mrs von Leinungen paused for a moment, considering how to explain. "Some people would say we're mad to be staying in a house that's built like a detective game. But that depends on what you mean by mad." She looked at them **intently**. "I'd say that the European Union is mad for paying fruit growers in Brandenburg to chop down orchards so that foreign fruit growers can keep importing their produce. I'd say that it's mad to feed cattle on animal **scraps** and turn them into cannibals, then serve the infected meat to unsuspecting consumers like you and me. And what's really mad is that we keep fighting wars, killing each other and polluting our planet."

"I completely agree," said Isy approvingly.

"You should **stand for** the Greens," added Amanda.

Mrs von Leinungen smiled. "In any case, it's just a bit of harmless fun. My friends and I like to indulge in a peaceful spot of Cluedo, and the fact that it's a detective game makes it all the more exciting. Gregor – or Reverend Green as we call him – took the trouble to convert the mill into a splendid English mansion, and we like to escape from our normal lives for a week or so and become Cluedo characters instead."

---

intent – konzentriert;
scraps – Essensreste;
to stand for – als Wahlkandidat antreten

She smoothed her **starched** white apron. "Today I'm playing the housekeeper, Mrs White."

"What about Dr Schley?" asked Amanda.

"Ursula Dorothee? She's taking a well-earned break from looking at teeth." Mrs von Leinungen chuckled and pointed to the broken plate. "That was supposed to be her dinner. She's a vegetarian."

She suddenly remembered that her visitors had some explaining to do. "Why are you here?"

"There's something important we have to tell you," said Isy. She paused and glanced around. "Is there a dustpan anywhere? We should probably sweep up the vegetables first." They hunted for runaway peas and rolling carrots, then Mrs von Leinungen made a salad while Isy and Amanda told her about the intruder in her apartment.

"And so we drew three conclusions: first, that the intruder was in possession of a key; second, that he knew his way around your apartment; and third, that he was looking for something but didn't find it because we walked in. I hope you're not cross with us for changing the locks," said Isy.

"On the contrary, I'm very grateful to you. I suspected that a certain someone would try to get into the apartment. This particular person is more **persistent** than I thought." Mrs von Leinungen garnished the tomatoes with some parsley. "I know exactly what he was after."

"Your will!" said Isy with a knowing nod.

---

to starch – stärken;
persistent – hartnäckig

Mrs von Leinungen smiled and shook her head. Then she asked after Otti and Lotti and made the girls some sandwiches to eat on the journey home. She phoned the mansion's chauffeur and gave them each a hug. "I'll be back in Berlin by the end of next week!"

"If you like, we can all play Cluedo when you're home," offered Isy. "We're Cluedo fans as well, you know." She grinned. "It's Amanda's favourite game."

It wasn't long before the tired friends were on their way back to the city in an old Rolls Royce. They **chomped** through their sandwiches and enjoyed the ride – the car was old, but it was a proper Rolls Royce, and they couldn't think of a grander way of travelling, except perhaps by flying carpet.

"This is the life," said Amanda happily.

"Are you really a chauffeur?" asked Isy when the driver dropped them off at the end of Gummy Bear's street.

"Only in the holidays," he admitted, putting his hand to his cap. "I spend the rest of the year torturing my pupils with physics."

The teacher chuckled and drove away.

"No one's ever going to believe what happened to us today," sighed Amanda. "First the Cluedo mansion, and then a real Rolls Royce!"

"Did you notice that Mrs von Leinungen didn't tell us his name?" asked Isy as they hurried to-

---

to chomp – mampfen

wards Gummy Bear's apartment to pick up Alfredo.

"Whose name?"

"The name of her relative. She didn't tell us what he was looking for either. And it doesn't explain the blood in the bathroom. I'm not finished with this investigation yet."

"Not finished?!" Amanda looked like she had been struck by lightning. "Wasn't today's debacle enough for you? Can't you accept that no one abducted Mrs von Leinungen? It was all a figment of your imagination. We wasted an evening in Brinkenbühl for no reason at all! Do you realize how frightened I was? I almost died of shock!"

"Fine, I was wrong," admitted Isy. "But at least Mrs von Leinungen is still alive! And you shouldn't be so trusting. Take a proper look around! This city is home to all kinds of criminals!"

Amanda looked around and came face-to-face with the headline news. 'Kidnapper Demands 250,000 Euros' screamed the newspapers in the kiosk opposite Gummy Bear's house.

The kidnapper had made contact. Things were beginning to hot up.

— 14 —

Nothing in particular happened the following day. After the recent excitement, Isy and Amanda were relieved to spend a few hours quietly grooming cats, topping up drinking bowls, and watering plants.

They raced through their duties, and Amanda didn't even object when Isy suggested that she should take care of Professor Pioschleck's mailbox and flowerpots on her own. In fact, she was positively in favour of the idea. She didn't want Isy sharing a single second of her precious time in Pio's apartment!

Her happiness would have been complete if her guru had been there to welcome her in person. Instead she was met by his housekeeper, who had packed her suitcase and was hoping to get to the Netherlands in time for her grandson's birth. The professor had returned to his main residence in the former FRG and was preparing to shoot the next episode of his show.

"It's the one about pumpkin pie. I need a new pumpkin, pronto!"

Isy was glad to be given a challenge that could be easily met. There was no shortage of pumpkins in October.

In fact, why couldn't Amanda buy one herself?

After feeding Gottfried the goldfish, they made their way to Wilmersdorf to take care of a Persian cat. Its elderly owner was on a sightseeing tour of

North Africa. Despite her advanced years, she was eager to further her cultural education and had decided to pursue her interest in Mozambican art. Her tomcat was called Wolodja, and his temperament was as dark as his fur.

Unlike Otti and Lotti, he paid no attention to his litter tray and did his business in the corner of the room. He had a tendency to hide under the sofa as soon as Isy and Amanda appeared. They rarely caught sight of him – but they could tell where he was by the smell.

They left Hohenzollerndamm station, walked to the apartment block and stepped into the elevator. "I'm going to ask for a pay rise if that stinking cat has **peed** on the carpet again," said Amanda. "I'm not the Good Samaritan!"

"You're telling me!" Isy burst out laughing. "But you've got to see it from Wolodja's point of view. His mistress has left him, he's scared of us, and he's terrified of Alfredo. It's very stressful!"

"It's very stressful *for me*!" muttered Amanda. "He's the most unfriendly cat I've ever known!" She marched out of the elevator and waited next to the burgundy front door while Isy hunted for the key.

Isy was tempted to speak out on behalf of Wolodja, but she decided to let the matter drop. Amanda had suffered enough already, and there was no point in causing an argument.

In fact, the strain on Amanda had been so great

---

to pee – pinkeln

that Isy, after sniffing the air in the hall, decided to clean up Wolodja's smelly protest by herself. She told her friend to go shopping and gave her three euros.

"Buy yourself a pumpkin," she said generously. "I'll manage on my own."

"Are you sure?" Amanda bounced up and down excitedly. "Does that mean I can go?"

The door slammed behind her. Isy smiled to herself and went into the kitchen to fetch some paper towels. She opened the windows, filled a bucket with water, added some disinfectant, grabbed a scrubbing brush, and set about eliminating Wolodja's mess. Sunshine streamed through the arched window on the upper level, dappling the floor with cheerful patches of colour like scattered autumn leaves. Alfredo lay down and soaked up the warmth. Isy preferred Wolodja's maisonette to all the other apartments on their list. The kitchen, bathroom, living room and dining room were on one level, and the bedrooms were on the storey above.

Sometimes she tried to imagine what her life would be like when she was older. Needless to say, she wanted to live in a cool apartment, and now she could picture it exactly: her dream apartment would look precisely like this.

For a while she allowed herself to indulge in rose-tinted visions of the future. She would race round Berlin in a bright yellow convertible, pursue a successful career as a court reporter or detective, go shopping in trendy boutiques, and meet Amanda in fashionable cafés. And then she would go home to her beautiful maisonette apartment to find her two children playing happily in their bedrooms while her husband cooked dinner in their shiny chrome kitchen. Naturally, her husband would be sporty and handsome as well!

She finished clearing Wolodja's mess and filled his bowl with water and cat food. It was time for a chat with the troublesome cat.

She went into the living room and knelt on the carpet. There was a large **gap** under the sofa, and Wolodja was sitting in the far right-hand corner. He had rolled himself up into a black ball and his yellow eyes were gleaming like two miniature moons in the darkness. This time he didn't hiss when he saw her, which was evidence of a **détente**. She talked to him in a gentle, comforting voice, and told him that his mistress wouldn't be away for long. Then she gave Alfredo some fresh water and drank a glass herself. When Amanda finally returned with a medium-sized orange pumpkin, Isy and Alfredo were already waiting in the hall.

Their final client of the day was Mrs Ober-Lippe. They hurried to the underground and were outside her apartment block within a quarter of an hour. Her mailbox contained two newspapers, a letter, a picture postcard, and lots of junk mail. The postcard showed **craggy** snow-capped mountains against a

---

gap – Spalt;
détente – Entspannung; craggy – zerklüftet

luminous blue sky. Amanda turned it over. "Dearest Lullula arborea, my precious **woodlark**," she read, giggling. "I hope you haven't forgotten this beautiful place. Do you remember how we kissed here for the first time all those years ago ..."

She was interrupted by frenzied barking. Alfredo was staring suspiciously at the jumble of blue plastic **curlers** that had appeared in the doorway of a neighbouring apartment. They were attached to the head of a plump red-haired woman who was looking at them mistrustfully. "What are you doing here?"

"We're Mrs Ober-Lippe's holiday angels," explained Isy. "She asked us to collect her mail."

"Did she ask you to read it aloud in the corridor?" the woman said cuttingly.

Amanda went bright red.

"The old dragon was **eavesdropping** on us!" she said indignantly as soon as they were safely inside Mrs Ober-Lippe's apartment.

"You've got to admit that she had a point," replied Isy, who was leafing through Mrs Ober-Lippe's newspaper in search of news about Josepha.

According to the article, the kidnapper had made contact with the family. He had communicated his demands in the usual fashion by cutting letters out of the newspaper and sticking them onto a blank sheet of paper. The police were still trying to work

---

woodlark – Heidelerche;
curler – Lockenwickler;
to eavesdrop – lauschen

out how he had found out about the inheritance, which no one had known about except Mrs Boskov herself. For the first time there was talk of a reward for information leading to Josepha's recovery: the amount on offer was 2000 euros.

"Two thousand euros!" grumbled Amanda, who was reading the article over Isy's shoulder. "That's nothing compared to the inheritance!"

The news about the reward was followed by a photograph of a smiling Detective Rose. He was said to be confident about the outcome of the investigation. The police dogs and heat-seeking cameras had found no sign of a body, which gave everyone cause for hope.

"Josepha is still alive," he told the reporter. "She's being **held to ransom**, and she's right here in one of the many thousands of apartments in Berlin. But we'll find her soon enough. The investigation has gained new impetus. We're on the point of cracking this case."

He explained to the reporter that volunteers from Josepha's school would be handing out photos of the missing girl throughout Berlin. "Hundreds of schoolchildren will be sacrificing a whole day of their holidays to help us find Josepha," he said proudly, and called on the citizens of the capital to help.

"That's tomorrow!" said Isy. "How are we going to find the time?"

---

to hold s.o. to ransom – jmdn. gegen Lösegeld festhalten

"Maybe they won't need us."

"Won't need us? Amanda, we promised!"

The tube was jam-packed with people. They balanced the pumpkin between them and listened to an impromptu performance by a couple of young musicians who were playing their violins in the middle of the carriage. It was a song from a musical. Informal concerts were nothing unusual on the Berlin underground, and in most cases the musicians were rewarded with coins, notes and a **smattering** of applause.

"We'll help out for just a couple of hours," whispered Isy.

"Isy, we won't have time! Grandma Braun will be expecting her shopping at eight, then there's Otti and Lotti. Leila will need her lettuce, and then I'll have to go to Pio's. We're supposed to feed Wolodja at twelve, and then we'll be off to Weissensee to water the plants. And what about Gottfried?" objected Amanda breathlessly.

"We'll have to get up earlier."

"Earlier?!"

"We can't **let** Josepha **down**! You should know how it feels to be let down by someone! What about your missing cash?"

"Who says I was going to let Josepha down?" protested Amanda, blushing.

The violinists struck up a classical melody. The holiday angels were so wrapped up in their argu-

---

smattering – ein klein wenig;
to let s.o. down – jmdn. im Stich lassen

ment that they nearly missed their stop. They jumped out at the last moment.

"Why are you always so difficult?" said Isy accusingly. "It's probably because you're a Taurus. They supposed to be incredibly stubborn."

Amanda ignored her. She was standing motionless on the platform, staring after the tube. The last carriage disappeared into the darkness of the tunnel. "Byeeee!" she shouted at the top of her voice.

The other passengers turned and stared at her.

"Who were you saying goodbye to?" asked Isy, puzzled.

"To the pumpkin, of course!" her friend replied furiously. Then the two of them fell about laughing.

— 15 —

There was something particularly special about the autumn break.

It was the last chance before winter to laze in the sun, **stroll** along kilometre after kilometre of golden sand in search of pretty shells, swim in the clear blue sea and eat lemon ice cream by the bucketful.

Of course, that was assuming that you weren't stuck in Germany.

Amanda was accustomed to spending the autumn break in Gran Canaria. Muttering under her

---

to stroll – schlendern

breath, she trudged unhappily through the mud and **drizzle** of the schoolyard.

She never wanted to spend the autumn break in Germany again; and she certainly never wanted to work in the holidays!

Isy was tired of hearing about it. She decided not to listen.

Her thoughts turned to Josepha Boskov. Amanda had no right to complain when one of their schoolmates was missing without **trace**.

Isy hoped that Detective Rose was right and that Josepha was being held in a normal apartment, and not in a cold, dank bunker, **well shaft** or underground hideout. She shuddered at the thought.

The holiday angels had spent the morning rushing from apartment to apartment. They had changed their clothes at the end of their final errand, but now they were sorry that their uniforms were stashed safely in their rucksacks: the curly wigs and long cloaks offered perfect protection against the wind and rain.

The school was buzzing with activity when they arrived. Isy and Amanda pushed their way up the steps and smiled at the familiar faces. The door to the **staff room** was open, and Trischi gave them a wave. He and Detective Rose were talking into a reporter's microphone.

---

drizzle – Nieselregen;
trace – Spur;
well shaft – Brunnenschacht;
staff room – Lehrerzimmer

They hurried to classroom 7a to collect their supply of pictures of the missing girl and posters designed by their schoolmates. The photocopier and printer were spitting out an endless stream of paper. They almost collided with Saskia and Binette in their hurry to get there.

"Oh, you're still alive, are you?" teased Sassi and Bini. "We haven't seen you in ages."

"We haven't seen you either!" Amanda rushed past and grabbed a stack of leaflets. Isy spotted Tannhäuser in the corner of the room. He was leaning over a laptop with Janho from the ninth grade and a few other boys from their class.

"They're trying to make contact with the kidnapper," explained Saskia, who had dyed her hair purple. "Who's this little fellow?" she asked, bending down to stroke Alfredo.

Isy smiled. "Don't you remember? He's Alfredo, Mr Rimpau's dog."

She hurried away to fetch her own stack of photos and posters.

By the time they left the building, it was raining heavily. They put up their hoods.

"It's rubbish weather for this kind of thing," sighed Sassi, wiping the raindrops from her nose. "What do you think about Mrs Boskov's money? She's supposed to have inherited half a million euros, and the kidnapper is demanding half. Do you think she'll pay?"

Isy shook her head. "I shouldn't think so. Not now that the police are involved."

"You know heaps about this sort of thing," said

Saskia admiringly. "Bini and I are going to distribute our flyers in Lafeyette. Department stores are always a good bet. We're going back to my place as soon as we've finished. My parents gave me "The Settlers IV" as a present. Do you want to come, too?"

"No, we've got to go to Karlshorst."

"Karlshorst? Whatever for?" chorused Sassi and Bini, surprised.

"Oh, nothing in particular," said Isy casually, cursing herself for not being more careful.

"Nothing in particular?" Bini gave Isy and Amanda a hard look. "I've called you three times since the start of the holidays. According to your parents, you're never at home."

"Parents always **exaggerate**," said Isy. "We've been earning a bit of money, that's all."

"Just a couple of odd jobs for a few VIPs," explained Amanda.

Sassi and Bini exchanged looks. "Such as who?"

"We can't tell you their names, but there's a certain famous professor who likes to cook …"

Sassi and Bini looked suitably impressed. "Seriously? Wow! That's amazing!"

Amanda nodded proudly. "And then there's a movie director who knows Maximilian Schell. Working with celebrities is brilliant."

"And which of your celebrities lives in Karlshorst?"

Amanda grinned. "Gottfried. That's his stage name."

---

exaggerate – übertreiben

"I know him!" exclaimed Sassi. "He's a pop star!"

"Actually, Gottfried is **mute**."

"Oh, I see. Catch you later!" The two girls waved and hurried off. A moment later they were deep in conversation.

"Look at them!" said Isy. "They'll be gossiping about us all day!"

Amanda followed her into a tram that was headed for Schöneweide station. They had originally planned to distribute their flyers at one of the mainline stations, but tourists and day-trippers weren't likely to know anything about the missing girl. In the end they had settled on Schöneweide. It was one of the busier stations en route to Gottfried in Karlshorst.

They got out of the tram, pushed through the crowds, and started distributing flyers outside the station. Most of the passers-by were eager to help. Some of them seemed genuinely worried about the missing girl. But one woman refused to take a flyer. "Her parents are foreigners!" she told Amanda angrily. "These **blasted** Boskovs and the rest of them have put me and my husband out of a job. I'll be damned if I'm going to help them!"

"Did you hear that?" The outraged Amanda stopped what she was doing and turned to Isy, who was sticking a poster of Josepha to a telegraph pole.

"I'm afraid so! What a bitter and twisted

---

mute – stumm;
blasted – verdammt

woman! She was **downright** xenophobic!" Her hood had fallen back and the wind swept through her damp hair. She checked that the poster was firmly attached, then **cocked her head** and looked at it intently. "Don't worry, Josepha. It won't be long now." The girl on the poster smiled back with watchful blackbird eyes.

They spent the next hour walking around the station and handing out photos. They were **drenched** to the skin and freezing cold, but they didn't let it drag them down. It felt good to be doing something for Josepha.

In fact, Isy was beginning to think that they should be doing more. She remembered how Tannhäuser had asked her whether she and Amanda were going to solve the case. He hadn't really meant it, of course, but Isy felt guilty about not taking the matter more seriously. They had been too busy worrying about their own problems …

"We should have got involved from the beginning," she said. They were in Gottfried's apartment in Karlshorst, and Isy was drying the dripping Alfredo with one of Mrs Knosalla's three plastic hair dryers. "We might have found her by now."

"**Come off it**, Isy! The police are doing everything they can to find Josepha. What makes you

---

downright – richtig;
to cock one's head – den Kopf zur Seite neigen;
to drench – durchnässen;
come off it! – nicht übertreiben!

think we'd do better?" replied Amanda from the kitchen where she was brewing a pot of herbal tea. She couldn't wait for her feet to warm up. "Sure, it would be nice to get the reward. We wouldn't have to leap out of bed at the crack of dawn and run **errands** all day. But quite frankly, the fiasco in Brinkenbühl was enough for me. Your obsession with criminals will be the death of us."

"It's our duty as good citizens to help the police. And anyway, we've survived up until now. You always look pretty pleased with yourself when you make the headlines at the end of the case!"

"Atisshoo!" sneezed Amanda. "I don't want to think about it!"

They both took a sip of tea. It tasted like straw, but at least it was hot. Under normal circumstances, they would never help themselves to the contents of a client's **pantry**, but on this occasion they made an exception. They were desperate for a hot drink and they fully intended to replace the missing teabags.

Mrs Knosalla wasn't especially wealthy, but she had a knack of winning competitions. Almost everything in the kitchen was present in duplicate: she had two toasters and two microwaves. There were three televisions and two stereos in the living room, plus an assortment of unattractive cushions, some paintings and some silver cups. The Japanese goldfish and her week at the beauty spa were two of the many prizes that she had won.

---

errand – Besorgung, Botengang; pantry – Speisekammer

"Did you see what Janho was doing earlier?" asked Isy, putting down her cup. "He and Tannhäuser were working on a laptop with a few other guys. They were trying to contact the kidnapper on the Internet."

"Was it working?"

"I don't suppose so. If anyone answers, the police will use their computer specialists to track them down. I'm sure the kidnapper knows that." They sat for a while in thoughtful silence, then it was time for them to go.

Next on the list was Neukölln, followed by Britz, but they stopped for a moment to chat to the goldfish first. They had promised to talk to him every day. The well-fed Gottfried was resting among the elegant greenery of his watery home. He listened to them gratefully with invisible goldfish ears.

"It's all right for him!" sighed Amanda. "I'd love to be relaxing in a tub of warm water!" She knocked gently on the side of the aquarium. "See you tomorrow, Mr Fish!"

Unfortunately for Amanda, she was forced to cancel her appointment with Gottfried. The next day she was laid up in bed. She had a headache and a sore throat, and her mother had smothered her in Vicks VapoRub.

"I'll be fine tomorrow," she **croaked** into the receiver. "Honestly, Isy, it's just a sore throat."

---

to croak – krächzen

Isy hoped to goodness that she was right. There was too much work for a single person.

"We're having a dinner party tonight," her mother had told her that morning. "You'd better not be late. It would be lovely if you could make some table decorations. You do them so nicely."

Isy gave in without a fight. Her frequent absences had got her into enough trouble lately. If only the dinner party could have been another night!

She ate her breakfast gloomily and tried to work out which of her errands she would have to leave out. It wouldn't be the end of the world if she neglected the greenhouses for twenty-four hours – she and Amanda had taken excellent care of plants until now. And Mrs Ober-Lippe's newspaper could spend the night in her mailbox for once. Professor Pioschleck had only asked them to deal with his mail and houseplants, so she could leave him out as well. Besides, Amanda had checked on the elegant penthouse the previous day. So that left the pets and Werner B. Braun's grandma in Berlin-Mitte.

Isy jumped up from the breakfast table in alarm. It was nearly eight o'clock! She was going to be late.

She quickly stuffed her hair into her wig and put on her fleecy cape. Then she emptied the basket of warm rolls into a plastic bag and added a bottle of milk from the fridge. Poor Benedikt would wonder what had happened to his breakfast.

She whistled for Alfredo and hurried towards

the station. When they got to the three maple trees in front of the supermarket, Alfredo stopped to sniff beneath the bright yellow foliage and cock his leg. Isy **tugged** on the leash, but he refused to be hurried.

It was quarter to nine by the time she finally arrived at apartment 1101 and hung the plastic bag on the yellow door. She hurried back to the elevator and was already racing towards the ground floor when it occurred to her that maybe she should have rung the bell and apologized. Wolfram B. Braun had said something about his grandmother not wanting to be disturbed, but Isy was worried that the old woman wouldn't realize that her shopping had been delivered. What if she had checked outside earlier and given up hope? The poor thing would be starving. And Isy and Amanda would be made to pay the price. The movie director didn't seem like someone who tolerated mistakes.

"We've got to go back," she told Alfredo. There was a gentle **whirring** noise as the elevator carried them smoothly to the eleventh story where the bag of shopping was still dangling above the green doormat of apartment 1101.

Isy decided to ring just once. If no one answered, Wolfram B. Braun's grandmother was probably still asleep, in which case she wouldn't have noticed the delay.

She was just about to put her finger on the

---

to tug – zerren;
to whirr – surren

buzzer when the door opened and a hand reached out to **swipe** the bag.

By the time Isy recovered her voice, the hand was gone, and the door was firmly closed. She heard the **patter** of bare feet on the floor.

Isy stared at the door in confusion. She almost wondered whether she had imagined it all.

There was no time that morning to reflect on the stroke of luck that had led Wolfram B. Braun's grandmother to choose precisely that moment to reach for her supplies. She administered Leila's vitamin drops and fresh lettuce, cleared up after Wolodja, and provided Fred, the cheerful canary, with some fresh **millet**. Then she got back on the bus to feed Gottfried some delicious water **fleas**. Finally, she bought a tin of Whiskas from a corner shop and hoped that Otti and Lotti wouldn't notice that it wasn't Chinese. Exhausted from her efforts, she called in on the **ailing** Amanda to make her report.

"Don't tell me that they actually ate Whiskas!" exclaimed Amanda in amazement. "And you saw the famous grandma?"

"I only saw her hand. She grabbed the bag like lightning!"

---

to swipe – *(hier)* hastig ergreifen;
patter – Trippeln;
millet – Hirse;
flea – Floh;
ailing – kränkelnd

Amanda's bedroom door opened and her mum waltzed in with a mug of hot lemon. She offered Isy a drink.

Isy blushed. "No, thank you. I'm just about to go. We're expecting visitors and mum asked me to make the table decorations." She always felt awkward in front of Mrs Bornstein. Amanda's mum was somehow different. For one thing, she was a good deal more glamorous than other mothers. On this occasion, she was in a hurry to get to the **beautician's**.

Amanda heaved a sigh of relief. She knocked the book off her bed and jumped up to fetch a cigarette.

"I'll tell her that it was you," she said. She took three puffs before stubbing it out. "It tastes awful," she said in disappointment.

"I thought you only smoked for show," said Isy, bewildered.

"I'm trying to lose weight. My jeans are too tight." Amanda reached under her pillow and pulled out a scrap of paper that was covered in sums. "Look, I've added everything up, and this is what it comes to. We've earned enough for the course already. From now on, every cent we earn belongs to you. Didn't you want to buy a scanner? Why don't–" She broke off and started coughing.

"You sound awful," said Isy, concerned.

"Nonsense! I'll be right as rain tomorrow!" Amanda took a mouthful of cough mixture from

---

beautician – Schönheitspfleger

the bottle by her bed, and smiled bravely. "You know I wouldn't let you down!"

"Make sure you get enough sleep," recommended Isy. "I'll see you tomorrow at Otti and Lotti's. I'll see to Werner B. Braun's grandma and Mrs Ober-Lippe's mailbox first."

Her mind was already working on something else. One of Amanda's questions had unsettled her, but she couldn't remember which. She **racked her brains** uneasily. She was sure that she had missed something important, but she couldn't think what.

She walked home and made the table decorations, still racking her brains. When she was finished, she was as puzzled as before.

Her eyes swept the glistening chestnuts and bright autumn leaves on the tablecloth. She had collected the materials for the decorations on her way home, and she knew her mother would be proud of her. But she wasn't any closer to solving the mystery.

— 16 —

That night Isy dreamt that she and Amanda were on holiday at the field centre in Altgrünheide.

Everyone in 7b was with them and they were celebrating with an amazing party. Suddenly Isy remembered Wolfram B. Braun's grandma: the old

---

to rack one's brains – sich den Kopf zerbrechen

lady was waiting for her shopping while she and Amanda were on a field trip in the countryside. The poor thing would be starving by now.

How long had she gone without food?

To Isy's horror, she couldn't remember when the trip had started. Gripped by panic, she tried to find Amanda, but the field centre was packed with people and her friend was nowhere to be seen.

"Amanda! Where are you, Amanda? We've got to go back to Berlin! Wolfram B. Braun's grandma needs her shopping! We'll buy some bread rolls at the bakery on the way!"

The next moment, she woke up with a start, heart pounding and forehead covered in sweat. The events of the previous day came flooding back to her. She had lain awake for ages, plagued by the thought that something had happened that deserved her attention; something that she had seen and **subconsciously** registered.

Yesterday at Amanda's, she had half-remembered something, but it was too **hazy**, too **fleeting** ...

I'll do everything in the same order as yesterday, decided Isy. *It might **jog my memory**.* Galvanized into action, she jumped out of bed and managed to hang the bag of rolls and milk on the bright yellow door before the appointed time of eight

---

subconsciously – im Unterbewussten;
hazy – schleierhaft;
fleeting – flüchtig;
to jog one's memory – dem Gedächtnis nachhelfen

o'clock. Then she sat on the floor beside Alfredro, hugged her knees and waited.

Isy couldn't help feeling slightly stupid. School holidays were supposed to be for lying in bed and reading crime novels, not **crouching** in the corridor of an apartment block and staring at a stranger's door.

Typical morning noises sounded from the other apartments: running taps, raised voices, loud music, the roar of a vacuum cleaner. Alfredo leaned his head affectionately on her shoulder. He wanted to be stroked. Isy tickled his chin. "You'll be home tomorrow," she whispered. "We're meeting your master at the airport."

Alfredo pricked his ears attentively. He felt wonderfully warm beside her.

Isy was going to miss Alfredo, although she suspected that Selma and her parents would be delighted to see the back of her four-legged friend.

Lost in thought, she hardly noticed when a door opened beside her. A young woman and her daughter stepped into the corridor. Isy couldn't understand why the kid was staring at her, but then she remembered about the angel outfit. The little girl had never seen an angel in the corridor, especially not an angel with a large grey dog. She smiled and the girl smiled back. "I'm Lia. We're going swimming!" she said happily.

"I'd like to go swimming, too," sighed Isy.

She listened as the footsteps faded away, then

---

to crouch – hocken, kauern

glanced at her watch and yawned. She had been keeping watch for fifteen minutes and her right leg was beginning to go to sleep. But Isy wasn't destined to wait much longer. A moment later, the yellow door opened and a delicate hand reached out to grab the shopping. The events of the previous day repeated themselves, and within seconds the door was firmly closed.

This time Isy had grasped the significance of what she had seen. The mystery was solved. Amanda was never going to believe it.

She hurried away from the apartment block and ran down the street. Soon the Alexanderplatz was behind her and she was speeding towards Mrs Ober-Lippe's apartment. Alfredo trotted patiently beside her. Isy wondered whether he went everywhere with Mr Rimpau, too.

"I bet you always go by car," she teased the schnauzer. She fetched Mrs Ober-Lippe's newspapers from the mailbox and placed them on the kitchen table by order of date. It was a relief to know that the grammar school teacher would be back from the United Kingdom tomorrow. Fred's parents, tortoise-lover Max, and the owners of the conservatory in Weissensee would be home soon as well. Thank goodness she and Amanda wouldn't be quite so overworked during the last few days of their break! Isy took a last, careful look at the apartment, then locked the door behind her, stuffed the junk mail into the rubbish bin, and put the excitable Alfredo on the leash.

Twenty minutes later they arrived in Charlottenburg. Isy was literally bursting to tell Amanda about her discovery. She couldn't wait to see her friend's reaction!

Unfortunately, there was no sign of Amanda, so Isy went up to the apartment and started without her. First she stroked Otti and Lotti, then she changed the litter tray. She had just started vacuuming the hall when Amanda banged on the door.

"Mum wanted to keep me in bed. I waited for her to go shopping, then ran out of the apartment!" she said breathlessly. "I'm determined to go to my cookery course tonight! How's it going so far?"

"Fine! I've made a discovery!" said Isy.

Amanda didn't seem in the least bit interested or surprised. She tossed away her jacket, but left her woolly scarf around her neck. Then she carried her containers of pre-cooked food into the kitchen. Meowing, Otti and Lotti **scampered** after her excitedly.

"Are you feeling better?" asked Isy. "Can you handle a shock?"

"Certainly not!" said Amanda firmly. A knob of butter was **sizzling** in her frying pan.

"Not even if it's connected to renowned movie director Wolfram B. Braun?"

"Seriously?" Amanda looked at her expectantly.

"You're never going to believe who's been eating all those bread rolls!"

"His grandmother, of course! Who else?"

---

to scamper – sich umhertummeln;
to sizzle – zischen, brutzeln

"She's definitely not his grandmother!"

"What?" exclaimed Amanda, staring at her blankly.

"I saw her hand! It was ... Well, it wasn't an old person's hand!"

"What's that supposed to mean? You only caught a glimpse of it!"

"I've seen it twice!"

"So what? You can't jump to conclusions without seeing her face! Beside, it doesn't prove anything."

"It proves that something **fishy** is going on."

"Oh God," groaned Amanda, raising her eyes to the ceiling in despair. "You'd better not start that again."

"I'm serious, Amanda! Wolfram B. Braun told us that his grandma needs physiotherapy! She's supposed to be too old and fragile to go out to the shops! Do you honestly think she's the type to wear bright blue nail varnish and funky silver rings?"

Isy swept a strand of hair out of her eyes. Sometimes Amanda could be infuriatingly slow.

"Don't you see what's going on here? Your famous director was lying through his teeth. She's not his grandma; she's his lover! Either she's too exhausted in the mornings to fetch her own breakfast or ..." She paused. "Or he's keeping her prisoner!"

"As a sex slave?" asked Amanda, giggling excitedly.

---

fishy – verdächtig

"Who knows? In any case, he's been **taking us for a ride**. To think that he lectured us for posing as holiday angels! What a **hypocrite**!" Isy took a deep breath. "If you ask me, we should punish him for laughing at us!"

There was a short silence. Then Amanda looked at her doubtfully. "What if you're wrong?"

"I'm not wrong! Why don't you see for yourself tomorrow morning? And before I forget: Mr Rimpau wants us to meet him from Tegel airport at 11.22."

"Do you think we'll have time?" asked Amanda sceptically. She caught a **whiff** of something burning and hurried back to the stove. Isy heard swearing and frantic stirring from the kitchen.

She was just putting away the vacuum cleaner when a strange scratching noise stopped her in her tracks. Someone was at the door! By the sounds of it, he or she didn't realize that the locks had been changed! Before Amanda could stop her, Isy grabbed the pan from the stove, tipped the wantons onto a plate, and hurried to the front door. She opened it suddenly and took a swing at the intruder.

For a second she stared into a pair of blue eyes, then her arm continued its trajectory and the stranger, still smiling disbelievingly, crumpled to the floor.

---

to take s.o. for a ride – jmdn. hinters Licht führen;
hypocrite – Heuchler;
whiff – Hauch

"It's Janho!" she told the shocked Amanda. "Fetch some water, quick!"

"Can't we have a single day without a major drama?" her friend replied weakly. Hands trembling, she hurried to fetch a glass of water, but Janho had opened his eyes. He sat up, **dazed**. "Where am I?"

"In heaven!" said Isy sarcastically. "We're your angels!" She looked at him sternly. "What are you doing here?"

"I was about to ask you the same," he said, groaning. "My aunt lives here. I'm Janho von Leinungen. Have we met before?"

"Of course we've met! But we didn't realize you were Mrs von Leinungen's **rotten** nephew," said Amanda, flashing him her most charming smile. Alfredo sniffed his shoes curiously.

"You shouldn't believe everything Aunt Gudrun says." Janho got up and rubbed the red patch on his forehead. "Thanks for the warm welcome! I suppose the two of you are taking care of Otti and Lotti while my crazy aunt looks for murderers in Brinkenbühl ..."

"Don't you like Cluedo?"

"I'm the one who taught her to play! I just wish she wasn't quite so obsessed. She and the other **crumblies** spend their holidays together in a replica Cluedo villa."

---

dazed – benommen;
rotten – mies;
crumbly *(slang)* – alter Knacker

"We know," said Amanda. "It's a fabulous place."

"It does your aunt a power of good," added Isy. She eyed Janho with interest and wondered whether he really took drugs. He was undeniably good-looking. Even the blood streaming out of his **nostrils** couldn't ruin the effect.

Embarrassed, he searched his pockets for a tissue.

"Sorry, I'm always getting nosebleeds. Some of them are pretty dramatic. It's my blue blood, I suppose." He grinned. "What's with the weird outfits?"

"It's our uniform. We're holiday angels. Incidentally, your aunt won't be home for another week."

"Perfect. I'll drop by with some flowers before she gets back."

The girls exchanged glances.

"I'm afraid that won't be possible. We had to change the locks. A family member entered the apartment without her permission and hid in the wardrobe while we were here," said Isy, smiling at him sweetly. "Of course, we tidied up the mess, including the blood in the bathroom. I'm pretty sure it was blue blood like yours. Maybe the intruder suffers from nosebleeds."

They waited in vain for their schoolmate to look embarrassed. He didn't flinch. Janho von Leinungen was cool as a cucumber.

"I wouldn't be surprised," he said casually. "My whole family is prone to nosebleeds – and **nosi-**

---

nostril – Nüster

ness, too, for that matter. But what makes you think it was one of us?"

Several apartments later, their conversation still revolved around the mysterious Janho.

"He wasn't **fazed** by anything," said Amanda, admiringly, while she replaced the missing teabags in Mrs Knosalla's tin. "I bet he's wondering who we are!"

"He must be dying of curiosity!"

"How did you guess that he was the intruder?"

"Instinct," said Isy modestly. "We need to find out what he was looking for."

"Count me out," said Amanda. "It's none of our business."

But Isy had decided that it was definitely her business. And it was also her business to find out who had been eating their bread rolls. A mystery woman was hiding on the other side of Wolfram B. Braun's bright yellow door, and tomorrow morning Isy was determined to unmask her.

— 17 —

Flight 116 was an overnight flight from New York to Frankfurt. There was nothing different or special about it, so it came as a complete surprise when the American Boeing was forced to abandon its usual

---

nosiness – Neugierde;
to be fazed – durcheinandergebracht werden

route just as it was approaching the dark frontier of the Atlantic Ocean. It was precisely 02.44, Central European Time.

The cause of the **disruption** was a small box covered in pretty lavender-coloured silk that was hidden under a window seat on the left-hand-side of the plane, four rows from the front in economy class. Most cosmetic cases contained nothing more sinister than an oval-shaped bar of English soap, but this one was ticking ominously.

At the time, no one could say for sure whether it was really a bomb, but the captain of the Boeing, forty-two-year-old Ronald W. Smith, had been trained not to take risks. Besides, he had just left his wife, daughter and a Labrador called Duke in Queens, New York, and they were counting on his return.

Isy was cleaning her teeth when she heard the news.

She took the receiver from a furious Benedikt, whose sleep had been interrupted by the persistent ringing of the phone. Amanda's hysterical voice sounded down the line: "Isy, have you heard? Mr Rimpau has been hijacked!"

Less than an hour later, Isy and Amanda were hurrying towards Tegel airport where Mr Rimpau had been scheduled to finish his ten-hour-and-twenty-two-minute flight from New York to Berlin via Frankfurt. The wind was picking up and they were relieved to reach the shelter of the terminal without being blown over.

---

disruption – Störung

As Isy had suspected, the airport was relatively quiet.

Rather than bother with Tegel, the TV crews and journalists had congregated in Frankfurt and New York. It was there that the real frenzy was taking place. Reporters were pushing and shoving in their eagerness to get the latest on the Boeing, which had landed in the hot desert winds of Riyadh airport and was sitting on the runway, while Arab gunmen in black masks **trained** their weapons on its silver fuselage.

There was a certain amount of pushing and shoving in Tegel as well, but only because a number of families had decided to take last-minute holidays in the sun. The kids were running wild while their despairing mothers tried to regain control.

They hesitated for a moment, unsure where to go, then headed for the check-in desks where long-suffering airline staff were issuing boarding cards and helping passengers lift their luggage onto the scales.

The two friends explained their dilemma to a young woman with blue earrings and an orange tan. She directed them to the opposite end of the terminal.

"The staff at the information desk will be able to help you."

They hurried past the row of shops selling newspapers, gifts and cosmetics. On passing a flower shop, they smelled the earthy perfume of fresh

---

to train – *(hier)* richten

chrysanthemums and ferns. They had planned to buy a yellow rose with a nice long stem to present to Mr Rimpau, and Amanda had generously offered to pay. Isy wondered whether her debtor had paid back the money. Of course, Amanda hadn't admitted that it was Ruky – the **feckless** car thief was still enjoying her protection.

"Maybe Mr Rimpau missed his flight," said Amanda for the third time that morning. Isy kept quiet. In her opinion, it didn't seem likely. Mr Rimpau was a punctual man who hated to be late.

There was a queue of people at the information desk. Isy deduced from the worried looks on their faces that they were friends or relatives of the German passengers aboard the hijacked Boeing. A few members of the crowd were professionally interested in the affair. They were on the lookout for new information – or for heartbreaking interviews with tearful relatives.

On seeing Isy and Amanda's outfits, the middle-aged woman at the desk eyed the pair critically, then asked if she could help.

"It's about Mr Rimpau, the crime writer," explained Isy in a confidential whisper. She seemed to be assuming that the woman was not only acquainted with Mr Rimpau's novels but rated them among her favourite books. "He flew to New York for a week and he was due to arrive here this morning."

"Are you family?"

---

feckless – wertlos

"Yes, I mean, no. At least, Alfredo is," said Isy, pointing to the schnauzer. The woman smiled.

"In that case, I'm afraid I can't help you."

"Can't you tell us whether he was on board?" asked Amanda. The woman shook her head apologetically.

"I'm afraid not. I can check the passenger list, but the information is confidential."

"But we're worried about him!" objected Amanda.

"I'm sorry," the woman said again. Her face had frozen into a permanent smile. "Those are the rules."

"We're wasting our time here," said Isy, giving Amanda a little **shove**. "Let's go."

They headed **despondently** towards the exit, but someone called them back. It was the man with a **crew cut** who had been standing next to them at the desk. They had mistaken him for a relative.

"Excuse me, ladies. Did you say that the crime writer Patrick Mortimer Rimpau was among the passengers?"

"Yes, but who are you?" asked Isy, taken aback.

"I'm Jo Scribbler – Scribbler by name, **scribbler** by nature." He grinned and showed them his press card. He was a reporter from one of the evening papers.

---

shove – Schubs;
despondent – verzweifelt;
crew cut – Bürstenschnitt;
scribbler – Kritzler

"So Rimpau was in New York, then? And you were looking after his dog, I assume?"

Isy and Amanda barely had time to nod before he asked the next question. "Is his wife with him?"

"She's in Rome."

Mr Scribbler nodded. "How about we sit down for a chat? We'll do a quick interview and I'll treat you to a snack. What will it be? A piece of cake or maybe a filled roll?"

No sooner had he said the word 'roll' than the two girls stared at each other in horror. They had forgotten to deliver the shopping to Berlin-Mitte. The hijacking had taken precedence over everything else.

"I'm sorry, but we're in a hurry," said Isy quickly. "I'm afraid we've got to go."

"What about a photo?" the reporter called after them. "We need a photo of you and the dog!"

A photographer appeared out of nowhere and pointed his camera at them. The flash went off and Isy thought he had finished, then he took another ten or eleven shots. While his colleague snapped frantically, the reporter took out his notebook. "Names and ages, please! And why are you wearing these extraordinary outfits? I'm sure our readers are dying to know!"

"I'm Julia Roberts!" shouted Isy.

"And I'm Madonna!" cried Amanda. "We're the hottest holiday angels in Berlin!"

They burst out laughing and ran away. Later, when they were safely on the bus, they realized their mistake. A photographer had taken their picture! That evening their faces would be plastered all over the papers. They couldn't believe how careless they had been.

"My parents will recognize us," wailed Amanda. "So will everyone at school! I can't stand it when they call us calamity queens!" Suddenly she cheered up. "Hang on, they won't even recognize us! They'll see a couple of angels, that's all!"

It was a good point. They kept forgetting that they were walking around in disguise. It didn't solve the problem of Wolfram B. Braun's shopping, though. They were an hour-and-a-half late already, and the bakery would have sold out of rolls. The only alternative was to go to the supermarket.

Isy headed to the bread counter and joined the queue of pensioners and anxious mothers, while Amanda fetched the milk. She came back with a **bulging** shopping bag. "What have you got there?" asked Isy, surprised.

Rather than answer, Amanda opened the bag and Isy **peeked** inside. In addition to the milk, Amanda had purchased a medium-sized round vegetable with tough orange skin. It was pumpkin number three.

"It's only a couple of days until Pio broadcasts his recipe," she said **gravely**.

They sped off in the direction of the apartment

---

to bulge – sich aufbauschen;
to peek – flüchtig gucken;
grave – ernsthaft

block where Wolfram B. Braun's grandmother had been waiting for her breakfast for the past two hours. Or was she really his grandmother?

To Isy's surprise, she realized that she didn't give a damn about apartment 1101. Compared to Mr Rimpau's hijacked plane, the question of who was consuming the rolls was unimportant. In a few days Wolfram B. Braun would be back from his shoot, and she and Amanda would never have to deliver his shopping again. She just hoped that Mr Rimpau and the other passengers would be free by then.

"Do you think we should ring the bell and apologize," asked Amanda as they ascended to the eleventh floor.

"We haven't got time," said Isy. "You never know, she might insist on us playing bridge with her or something. I bought a slice of cherry tart. That should keep her happy."

"Fine. We'll leave the shopping on the door and get out of here," said Amanda in relief.

They stepped out of the elevator and **crept** to apartment 1101. As usual, the green mat was spotless. Isy put her ear to the bright yellow door and listened. There was silence in the apartment. She hung the shopping bag on the chrome doorknob. It was time to attend to their other clients who would be desperate for attention by now.

"Let's feed Wolodja first," proposed Isy. Suddenly the door to apartment 1101 opened noiselessly

---

to creep/crept/crept – schleichen, kriechen

behind them and a hand reached out for the bag. Isy put a finger to her lips and tugged on Amanda's jacket. She pointed to the hand. At last Amanda could see for herself that she was telling the truth. There was no way on earth that the hand belonged to Wolfram B. Braun's grandmother.

Amanda stared incredulously at the delicate fingers, bright blue nail varnish, shiny silver rings, slim wrist and blue-and-yellow friendship bracelet. Isy desperately wanted to laugh. The friendship bracelet was the final, **hilarious** touch.

The movie director's grandmother was surely the hippest old lady in town. Whoever heard of a pensioner with a blue-and-yellow… Isy froze. There was something significant about the bracelet. Hadn't someone mentioned a blue-and-yellow friendship bracelet at school?

Isy didn't have time to process the mind-blowing revelation. Darting forward, she grabbed the hand. Her fingers gripped the slender wrist like a **clamp**. Someone screamed in pain, then a startled face appeared at the door. It was exactly the face that Isy had been picturing for the last three seconds.

"Hello Josepha," she said warmly. "Can we come in?"

---

hilarious – heiter;
clamp – Schraubzwinge

— 18 —

Isy's mind went back to a bitterly cold December morning three years ago. She and her mother were going out somewhere. They had just left the apartment when Isy dashed back inside **on the pretext** of fetching her gloves.

She charged up the steps, tore open the door, stormed into the bedroom, and grabbed the key to the wardrobe. Heart pounding, she turned it in the lock. This was the moment she had been waiting for! She stared at the mountain of Christmas presents. Her intention wasn't to open them (Christmas Eve wouldn't be Christmas Eve without surprises!) but she was dying to pick them up and run her fingers over the wrapping paper. It was a wonderful way of heightening the suspense.

No sooner had she reached for the first parcel than a hand grabbed her shoulder. It gave Isy the shock of her life. She whipped round to see her well-meaning neighbour who was checking the apartment for burglars, having spotted the open door. Isy's expression at that moment was one of sheer, **unmitigated** terror.

She was reminded of the episode by Josepha's horrified face.

"Who are you?"

"Isy and Amanda from 7b."

"The calamity queens?" asked Josepha.

---

on the pretext – unter dem Vorwand;
unmitigated – ungemindert

"Exactly!" said Isy, taking off her wig. "How did you get here? The whole city is looking for you. The police are searching high and low!"

"They're using police dogs and Tornado jets to find you!" Amanda was staring at Josepha as if she couldn't believe it was her. "Don't you realize that your mother is sick with worry? She's never going to believe that you've been stuffing your face with bread rolls!"

Josepha bit her lip and stayed quiet.

"It's all right – you can tell us what's happening," said Isy. "We're here to help!"

"In that case, you can start by leaving me alone!"

Josepha's tone was unmistakably hostile. Isy and Amanda stared at her in disbelief. She was still in her blue pyjamas.

Isy decided that the poor girl didn't know what she was saying. She was probably still in shock.

"You're free!" she told her gently. "There's nothing to stop you going home. You can leave right away if you like."

"We'll take you straight to your mother," said Amanda. "She's offering a reward."

"Leave me alone!" snapped Josepha. "Don't you get it? You're ruining everything!"

A **baffled** silence descended on the room. Isy and Amanda had no idea what to make of the situation. What was Josepha talking about? What exactly did she think they were ruining? Something fell to the

---

baffled – verwirrt

floor with a **thud**. It was Amanda's pumpkin. She sat down heavily on the director's chair.

"Have you told Mr Braun that you're hiding in his apartment?" she asked crossly.

"Of course she has!" said Isy, looking scornfully at Josepha. "I'm afraid you'll have to kiss goodbye to your movie career, Amanda. Wolfram B. Braun and Josepha are **in cahoots**! They're after Mrs Boskov's money! Your famous movie director is a thief!"

She eyed the green sofa where Alfredo was lolling luxuriously. Judging by the blankets and cushions, Josepha had been sleeping in the living room.

Amanda swallowed. She couldn't believe that Wolfram B. Braun was a thief. "He can't be!"

"Ask Josepha! Maybe she'll tell you about her accomplice!"

Josepha had no intention of saying anything. Huddled in her dressing gown, she was staring out of the window. Her lovely eyes looked **listless** and dull. Isy wondered whether she was ill. It couldn't be healthy to be locked up inside. "Are you all right? Do you need a doctor?"

Josepha ignored her, but Isy refused to give up. "You're not even locked in! The police think you're being held for ransom, but you could have left **at the drop of a hat**!"

---

thud – dumpfer Schlag;
to be in cahoots – unter einer Decke stecken;
listless – teilnahmslos; at the drop of a hat – sofort

"The whole school has been looking for you. We sacrificed a day of our holidays to hand out flyers and photos," **chimed in** Amanda accusingly. "It was pouring with rain! I caught a cold because of you."

She coughed melodramatically to emphasize her point. To her disappointment, Josepha didn't seem the least bit sorry.

Isy was examining the stack of books beside the sofa. It was interesting to see Josepha's taste in books.

"I didn't realize that you were a bookworm like me. Have you finished them all?"

"I know them practically off by heart! I would have died of boredom otherwise."

Amanda pointed to the bread rolls. "Don't tell me you've eaten nothing but bread rolls?" she asked, looking enviously at Josepha's slender waist.

"I'm allergic to **preservatives** and I don't have much of an appetite. Besides, the kitchen has been **dismantled**, and there's nowhere to cook. I wasn't starving or anything. There was even a slice of cherry tart today." Josepha puffed on a cigarette. "Bread and milk are enough to survive on – for a short while, at least."

"What do you know about your abductor?" enquired Isy. The question was met with stony silence.

---

to chime in – sich in ein Gespräch einmischen;
preservative – Konservierungsmittel;
to dismantle – abbauen

Isy could see that Josepha wasn't going to talk to them. She decided to squeeze the information out of her instead.

"OK, Amanda, you'd better call Detective Rose. You've got his number, haven't you?"

Amanda stared back at her, confused.

But the tactic had the desired effect.

Josepha whirled round in panic. "Don't call the police," she implored them in a whisper. "Whatever you do, please don't call the police."

"Fine," said Isy, nodding in satisfaction. "We won't call the police, provided that you tell us what's going on. You'd better hurry because we don't have much time. And open the window – you need some fresh air!"

"I can't open the windows until after dark. I don't want anyone to see me."

"So you admit to being in cahoots with Wolfram B. Braun?"

"I've never heard of him!"

"He's a famous director!" said Amanda, livening up immediately.

"He told us that he lives here," explained Isy. "Tall, early forties, brown hair …"

"You mean, Lothar! Lothar Loll!"

Josepha told them that she and Lothar had met by chance in the **laundry** of the Boskovs' apartment block. Lothar had put his washing in the machine next to hers and offered her a cigarette. They had chatted for a while, and she had opened up to

---

laundry – *(hier)* Waschküche

him because he was a fan of Bosnia, too. On hearing that she wanted to return to her homeland, Lothar had come up with an idea that would enable her to escape for good. This time the police wouldn't be able to return her to her mother.

Lothar had promised to help her vanish without trace. The plan was for her to hide in empty apartments while he provided her with food and supplies. According to Josepha, her living conditions hadn't been so spartan at the beginning. Lothar had only hired the holiday angels for a short period because he was flying to Bosnia to make contact with her father.

"He told me about you. He said the shopping would be delivered by two little idiots who think they're really smart." Josepha smiled at them apologetically. "He thought you were too dumb to **catch on**."

Isy could scarcely believe her ears. What a cheek! She was pleased to see that Amanda, who had been fooled by the director, had blushed a shade of geranium-red.

"He'll be back by Halloween, and then I'm getting a **makeover**: new papers, a new haircut, new lips and a new nose. No one will ever recognize me!"

"A new nose! How cool!" gasped Amanda, but Isy tapped her head to indicate that Josepha was mad.

---

to catch on – kapieren;
makeover – Renovierung, alles neu

"Who's going to pay for it? I don't suppose Lothar is a millionaire!"

"He'll take care of it. He's borrowing some money from a friend," replied Josepha, fiddling nervously with her friendship bracelet. "Janho owes me a bit of cash as well. But Lothar reckons my dad will pay half."

"Maybe you should have asked him first."

"I don't know where he lives. I think he's moved."

"I know exactly where you can find your dad. He's staying with your mother in Berlin."

Josepha wrinkled her nose **contemptuously** and snorted in disbelief.

"Lothar was lying to you," said Isy solemnly. "Don't you have a phone?"

"Not any more. The kitchen is empty as well. The whole apartment is practically empty – except for the sofa, the desk and the chair."

"I see what he was up to," **snarled** Isy. "I bet you don't have a television or a radio either! Your darling Lothar didn't want you to see your parents crying their eyes out on TV!"

"Your mum is upset because the kidnapper is demanding half of her inheritance. That's 250,000 euros you know," said Amanda. "At least, that's what it says in the papers."

Josepha's laughter sounded strangely hysterical. She lit another cigarette. "Inheritance? You've got

---

contemptuous – verächtlich;
to snarl – knurren

to be joking! We're ordinary immigrants! We're poor. I knew you were lying!"

"But it's true! Your mother inherited a house last spring."

"Aunt Olga's old house? It isn't worth a cent!"

"Not in your opinion, but someone clearly thought differently." Isy looked impatiently at her watch, knowing that their other clients were waiting. She had to make Josepha see sense.

"I only met him by chance," the dark-eyed girl muttered helplessly. "We were in the laundry together."

"Coincidences are easy to arrange," said Isy, taking Josepha's hand. "It's always like that in detective stories. He must have known where to find you. He knew about you in advance!"

Josepha stood up with a jolt. "I want to speak to my dad."

"No problem," said Amanda, tossing her bright pink mobile across the room. Isy reached out and caught it just in time.

"Are you crazy? The police will be monitoring his calls! Do you want to get us arrested?"

"Maybe it's for the best!" Amanda reached into her bag and reapplied her lipstick. "Think of the reward! Besides, we didn't kidnap Josepha; we found her! The police will be grateful!"

"You promised not to call the police!" protested Josepha.

Isy nodded. "We made a promise, Amanda. Besides, the police would want to know what we were doing in the apartment. They'd tell our parents everything, and it could be really awkward, especially for you."

"What about the reward? Do you mean we won't get the money?" asked Amanda indignantly.

"Is that what you're worried about? For heavens sake, Amanda, we need to get Josepha to safety!"

"Why doesn't she just go home?"

"What am I supposed to tell my mum," wailed Josepha. "And anyway, Lothar knows where I live. If your suspicions are right, he'll..."

"Exactly. You know too much already. It's probably safer if you don't go home," decided Isy. "We'll hide you somewhere until Lothar has been arrested. When did he say he was coming? He asked us to keep delivering the shopping until the end of the month."

Josepha nodded. "He promised to meet me here at four o'clock on Halloween. He told me not to open the door to anyone before then."

"Perfect. We'll catch the villain as soon as he shows up!"

"What do you mean, 'we'?" protested Amanda.

"I mean the two little idiots who think they're really smart! He'll be sorry he underestimated us when we hand him over to Detective Rose. It'll be an early Christmas present from us to the police!" said Isy, grinning all over her face. "In the meantime, Josepha will have to hide in one of the apartments."

"How's that supposed to work? The owners will be home soon!"

"One of them isn't due back for a while longer.

He's working on a special pumpkin recipe for a certain Amanda Bornstein."

"I'm not letting you use Pio's apartment!" exclaimed an outraged Amanda. "It's out of the question! We can argue about it until the moon comes out for all I care!"

— 19 —

The moon came out very early that evening. It settled over Charlottenburg like a luminous grapefruit.

Otti and Lotti had finally finished eating. They stretched out contentedly. They had never had to wait so long for food and attention.

Sighing with exhaustion, Isy tickled their furry tummies. She was feeling the strain of Mr Rimpau's hijacking, Josepha's sudden appearance, and her fight with Amanda, who had been horrified at the idea of using Pio's apartment.

"Josepha will fill the place with her stinking smoke," she had said.

Amanda had eventually **caved in** – but only after Josepha had undertaken not to smoke in the apartment. The arrangement was only temporary and Isy had promised to come up with another solution for the following night. Deep down, she agreed with Amanda: it was wrong to abuse their clients' trust.

---

to cave in – *(hier)* nachgeben

In fact, Isy had a nasty feeling that she was out of her depth. Josepha's re-appearance was serious stuff. It was frightening to think that she and Amanda were the only ones who knew where she was. Everyone in Berlin was looking for her, and her parents were desperate for news. Was it wrong not to tell them? Were they doing the right thing by **prolonging** their anxiety? She and Amanda had been arguing about it all day.

They had argued all the way to Professor Pioschleck's penthouse. Dressed in Amanda's wig, glasses and cape, Josepha had looked completely unrecognizable. She had sat between them in the train without saying a word. They had still been arguing when they visited Wolodja in Wilmersdorf, Gottfried in Karlshorst and the conservatory in Britz. The quarrel had been no closer to being resolved by the time they had arrived at Max's apartment to give Leila her last dose of vitamin drops and scrawl a message in bright red lipstick on the mirror in the hall: "Welcome home! Remember to tidy your socks!" The debate had even continued throughout their conversation with Fred the canary in Neukölln.

At last, as the spicy smell of chop suey filled Mrs von Leinungen's kitchen, Amanda and Isy realized that they were too tired to argue anymore.

"The prickly Detective Rose will be furious with us," predicted Amanda **glumly**. "So will everyone else."

---

to prolong – verlängern; glum – missmutig

She gave the leftover chop suey a half-hearted stir. "The cats have eaten enough already. Would you like some?"

Isy nodded. They divided the meal between the two of them.

"Delicious!" said Isy. "I've never been to a Chinese restaurant. We hardly ever go out for meals. My parents think it's too expensive."

"You'll have plenty of money soon," replied Amanda, **beaming** at her brightly. For a moment they enjoyed the truce.

Then Isy said **pleadingly**, "There's no need to feel guilty, Mandi. No one will blame us for what we're doing when they see the end result! If Detective Rose and the others were in our shoes, they'd do exactly the same." She looked at her friend's worried face. "I know what you're thinking. You're imagining how happy everyone would be if Josepha were at home with her parents. The chief of police would shake us by the hand, and it would all be **hunky dory** – except for the fact that Lothar would still be on the loose!"

"I could pay for my cookery course straight away if we had the reward." Amanda **twirled** her fork nervously. "I don't understand why a famous director who's worked with Maximilian Schell would get mixed up in kidnapping and extortion."

---

to beam – strahlen;
to plead – betteln;
hunky dory *(slang)* – prima;
to twirl – zwirbeln

"For goodness sake, Amanda, he's not a director! He doesn't make films! He's a criminal!" said Isy, laughing in spite of it all.

Amanda washed up and watered the myrtle, while Isy gave Otti and Lotti some fresh water, and fetched their coats.

"Josepha is safe, and that's what's important," she told her friend. "No one can accuse us of acting irresponsibly. By getting Josepha out of the apartment, we probably saved her life. There's no telling what Lothar Loll would have done to her when he finally got his money. He might not have been intending to let her live, after all."

Amanda's eyes widened in horror.

"In any case," continued Isy hurriedly, "people can say what they like, but we're the ones who found her and got her out of danger. We need to find out why Loll has access to so many empty flats and how he came to know about Mrs Boskov's inheritance. And then we can **nab** him!"

"So long as you promise that we won't be collaring him on our own!" Amanda said stubbornly.

"Fine," promised Isy, locking the door behind them in relief. They caught their final bus of the day and sat back as the driver took them from the bright lights and **bustle** of West Berlin to the not-so-bright-and-bustling East. They wanted to watch the news at Isy's place and find out what had happened about the hijacking. They had listened to the

---

to nab – schnappen;
bustle – Geschäftigkeit

radio at various points in the day, but there hadn't been any new developments. The hijacked plane was still sitting on the tarmac in Riyadh.

Isy was just opening the front door when someone materialized noiselessly in the door of the next apartment. It was the neighbour who had caught her snooping in the wardrobe.

"Hello!" he said warmly. "You're the first one home, I see. I'm afraid you missed your visitor."

"My parents are visiting friends and Benedikt is on a field trip. Who was it?"

"A man – early forties, tall, dark hair. An acquaintance of yours, perhaps?"

"Probably," said Isy. "Thanks for letting me know."

The two friends disappeared into the apartment and made straight for the TV. They collapsed onto the sofa.

"Your neighbour doesn't miss much, does he?" said Amanda, grinning.

Isy nodded and blushed at the memory of the December morning. "He used to work for the Stasi. He's probably just bored."

She ran to the kitchen to fetch some snacks and came back armed with tacos and crisps.

The news hadn't started, so they sat through a stream of **commercials** and helped themselves to nibbles.

Isy was thinking about Josepha and the blue-and-yellow friendship bracelet. Had Janho really

---

commercial – Werbespot

given it to her? And why did he owe her money? What was going on between Josepha and Janho? Were they friends?

She glanced at the television and caught the end of a commercial for wool. It was followed by an advertisement for home security. Isy thought uneasily about their mysterious visitor. Amanda seemed to share her concern. "Who do you think it was?"

"I don't know … Someone calling for Benni, perhaps."

"I thought you said he was on a field trip."

Isy tried to recall the man's description.

"I'll spare your grey cells some effort," said Amanda. She slid nervously onto the floor. "It was him, all right. Early forties, tall, dark hair… He must have found out your address and come to get Josepha."

"Don't be ridiculous! How could he find out my address when he doesn't know our real names? You know it's not possible!"

"He must have found out where you live," insisted Amanda. The empty crisp packet fell off her **lap**, scattering fragments of fried potato across the carpet.

"He's capable of anything! He was probably spying on us."

It seemed unlikely that Lothar Loll would be spying on them, but Isy couldn't disprove it. It was one-nil to Amanda.

---

lap – Schoß

"You'll make a good detective yet," said Isy approvingly. They shoved the heavy chest of drawers across the hall and barricaded the door. It would keep them safe until the police arrived. And Alfredo was with them, thank goodness.

The news had started by the time they returned to the sofa.

Sitting on the runway of the Saudi Arabian airport was the gleaming silver Boeing. The reporter was calmly explaining that the Saudi Arabian government was negotiating with a group of terrorists from Yemen. Isy and Amanda stared at the screen without speaking. Mr Rimpau was on the other side of one of those tiny windows. They wondered what he was doing. Was he thinking about his family and his dog? Was he offering whispered words of comfort to the other hostages? Was he taking notes for his next novel? Was he dreaming of his release or of a whisky on the rocks? Was he planning a daring attack on the hijackers? Or was he sitting in silent prayer?

"We should light a candle for him," said Amanda.

Isy fetched a tealight and tried to light it. She broke the first couple of matches, then the flame went out before it reached the **wick**. In the end, she managed to light it, and they stood in front of the little flame, overcome with emotion. Alfredo joined them.

"To Mr Rimpau's safe return," said Isy solemn-

---

wick – Docht

ly, her voice wavering as uncertainly as the flame. Amanda let out a little **sob**. At that moment, the doorbell rang.

Isy and Amanda jumped a mile and stared at each other in horror. He was back!

Their courage suddenly failed them. They hardly dared breathe. For a few **interminable** seconds they were **rooted** to the spot. Alfredo's barking brought them to their senses. Isy was relieved that the schnauzer was still with them. Dogs were always useful when there were criminals on the loose. It suddenly occurred to her that the visitor might not be Lothar Loll after all. They tiptoed into the hall, then Isy, helped by Amanda, clambered onto the chest of drawers and peered through the spy-hole.

"Can you see anything?" whispered Amanda.

"Yes," hissed Isy. "A yellow cravat!"

"A yellow cravat!" Amanda looked like she was about to faint. "Isy, it's him!"

The doorbell rang again, this time more persistently, and Alfredo howled. The sound of his barking was enough to give anyone earache. He **pawed** furiously at the chest of drawers, desperate to get to the person on the other side of the door.

"We'll have to call the police," decided Isy, reaching for the phone. Suddenly she froze and stopped

---

sob – Schluchzer;
interminable – endlos;
rooted – angewurzelt;
to paw – mit den Pfoten scharren

dialling. What was that? She wondered whether her ears were playing tricks on her.

"Calm down, old boy! That's right, Alfredo, it's me! Why won't those funny girls let me in?"

– 20 –

He's trying to trick us, thought Isy. *It can't be Mr Rimpau. The real Mr Rimpau is in Saudi Arabia!*

Before she could warn Amanda, the door broke open with an almighty bang and the chest of drawers flew backwards as if it were made of cardboard. Wolfram B. Braun, alias Lothar Loll, was standing in the hall. She saw a yellow cravat and an ugly looking **submachine gun**. It was pointing at her chest. Lothar Loll scanned the hall.

"Where's Josepha?" he asked coldly.

"Run for your life, Amanda!" cried Isy, screaming and screaming.

When she next opened her eyes, her mother was standing at her bedside in a patterned nightdress. She was stroking Isy's hair. The bedside light was on and Isy could hear her father in the kitchen.

"What happened?" she asked, confused.

"You were having a nightmare, darling. We heard you screaming in your sleep. Your father is making some herbal tea to calm your nerves."

"I don't want any tea!" She sat up in bed and stared at the **rug**. "Where's Alfredo?"

---

submachine gun – Maschinenpistole; rug – Läufer

"I thought Mr Rimpau collected him yesterday evening."

"Mr Rimpau?"

"Don't you remember? You told us that Mr Rimpau came to collect Alfredo last night." Her mother looked at her anxiously. "Is something worrying you, Isolde?"

"Mr Braun broke into the apartment and told me to hand over Josepha. He had a submachine gun!"

"Who's Mr Braun?"

"The kidnapper, of course!"

"Don't tell me you're mixed up in this business about the missing girl!"

"Of course not!" Isy slumped back into bed. Her head was starting to clear and her memory was coming back to her. Panicking, she realized that she had almost told her mother the truth about Josepha.

"It's nothing, mum. Just a bad dream, that's all. Go back to bed," she said sleepily, rolling into her sleeping position and waiting for her mother to leave the room.

"It's about time you tidied up," murmured Mrs Schütze, picking up a few books from the floor. "You're too busy for your own good. I've never seen such bags under anyone's eyes!" She closed the door **reproachfully**.

Isy waited for a second, then rolled onto her back and gazed into the darkness. It was her second nightmare that week. She would never have

---

reproachful – vorwurfsvoll

thought that school holidays could be so stressful. The whole business with Josepha had been bad enough, but then Mr Rimpau had turned up at the door. He was a tall man with dark hair who could easily pass for a forty-year-old. It was no wonder that Isy had been having bad dreams!

She and Amanda had **hauled** the heavy chest of drawers away from the door and welcomed a suspicious Mr Rimpau. Luckily, he had been so touched by Alfredo's excitement and by the candle burning in his honour that he hadn't asked any awkward questions. Besides, Isy and Amanda had hovered around him like **pesky** mosquitoes, demanding to know where he had been, why he wasn't in Riyadh, and how long he had been home.

As it turned out, Mr Rimpau had landed at half-past-eleven at Tegel airport and had waited **in vain** for Alfredo and the girls. He hadn't boarded the **ill-fated** flight from New York to Frankfurt because he wanted to spend a day shopping in London. He had left New York twenty-four hours earlier than planned and flown to Tegel via London Heathrow.

It was a decision that had saved him a good deal of stress. Instead of trembling for his life on a hijacked Boeing, he had bought himself a new silk cravat from a luxury shop in Bond Street. He hadn't forgotten his holiday angels either. Isy and

---

to haul – *(hier)* wuchten;
pesky – lästig;
in vain – umsonst;
ill-fated – unselig

Amanda each received a beautifully wrapped box containing a heavy glass sphere. Suspended in the glass was a delicate **thistle** with beautiful petals. Isy's was blue; Amanda's was yellow. They were thrilled.

"Wow! How did you know that we collect **paperweights**?"

Mr Rimpau had also brought a copy of the evening newspaper. The two girls and Alfredo were pictured on page two. The article was headlined: "Rimpau in Riyadh? Two lovely little angels and their canine friend Alfredo pray for crime writer's life!"

He had shown them the article and frowned. "Were you trying to make my wife jealous?"

She and Amanda had explained how a reporter called Jo Scribbler had tricked them into having their photo taken. Mr Rimpau had listened sympathetically: he was all too familiar with the underhand tactics of the press.

Isy turned over again in bed, remembering her nightmare. Thank goodness the man at the door had been Mr Rimpau and not Lothar Loll! She was almost ready to laugh at her terrifying dream. The idea of a bogus movie director with a submachine gun was too ridiculous for words! Nonetheless, she still felt anxious. The **nagging** feeling had started last night while she was trying to get to sleep. Was

---

thistle – Distel;
paperweight – Briefbeschwerer;
to nag – *(hier)* bedrängen

she worried about Josepha? Or was she worried about where they were going to hide Josepha over the coming days?

To add to her problems, she had to find someone to help them with Lothar Loll. It definitely couldn't be a grown-up. Grown-ups were too faint-hearted to hunt criminals by themselves. They prided themselves on being 'sensible', but really they weren't brave enough to take on anyone without the backing of the police. Even Mr Rimpau, acclaimed author of hard-boiled detective fiction, would be too **timid** to help them.

The only realistic candidates were Tannhäuser and Gummy Bear. They were **game** for anything, especially if danger was involved. She would give them a call tomorrow and **concoct** a convincing story. Josepha's identity had to be protected at all costs.

Holding her breath, Isy strained her ears for noise, but the voices in the kitchen had fallen silent. Her parents had gone back to bed. Isy had seen the look of concern on her mother's face, but there was nothing she could do to reassure her until they had **collared** Lothar Loll.

She had a sudden urge to call Amanda. They were in this mess in the first place because Amanda had lent Ruky her savings. But Bumblebee was

---

timid – schüchtern;
to be game for s.th. – für etwas zu haben sein;
to concoct – *(hier)* erfinden;
to collar – erwischen

probably sound asleep in her lovely warm bed, while Isy tossed and turned restlessly. If only she could think of somewhere for Josepha to hide! It didn't matter where, provided that no one recognized her. The trouble was, Josepha's face was plastered all over Berlin. They were searching for her everywhere!

After racking her brains for an eternity, she dozed off in exhaustion. This time she was blessed with a happy and helpful dream.

Isy had a vision of a place where no one would think of looking for Josepha. It was a lovely big house full of people who would protect her without realizing who she was.

Isy woke up with a huge weight off her mind. She knew exactly what to do.

— 21 —

That morning journalists across the globe were reporting the successful release of the hostages in Riyadh. The hijackers had given themselves up overnight. Thankfully, it hadn't been necessary to storm the aircraft.

Isy and Amanda listened to the news with relief, then made their way to Pio's penthouse where Josepha was waiting.

They had made her some breakfast: a boiled egg, a couple of **scrumptious** cheese rolls and some

---

scrumptious – köstlich

oranges. As soon as they sniffed the air in Professor Pioschleck's hallway, they knew that Josepha had broken her word. Amanda's feelings towards her went from lukewarm to frosty. She slammed the food parcel onto the breakfast bar and opened the window without a word.

"Are you any good at Cluedo?" asked Isy while Josepha **bolted down** her breakfast.

"What's Cluedo?"

"A game." Isy opened the board and set up the pieces. "I'll show you how to play."

In the background, the **aggrieved** Amanda was removing all traces of Josepha's presence from the **revered** professor's apartment. Meanwhile, Isy explained the rules. They played a couple of rounds and Josepha won on both occasions.

"Excellent," said Isy with a sigh of satisfaction. "You'll be a hit at the mill."

She pulled a long length of chequered fabric from her rucksack and draped it over Josepha's head. It was the Turkish disguise that she and Amanda had worn last spring while they were following a bird thief. "You look like a real Muslim," she said admiringly.

"I *am* a real Muslim," said Josepha with pride.

"What does your religion say about smoking?" snapped Amanda. She slid a pair of sunglasses onto Josepha's nose to complete the disguise.

---

to bolt down – verschlingen;
aggrieved – gekränkt;
to revere – verehren

"I could ask the same of you!" retorted Josepha.

"Come on, we'll miss the bus to Brinkenbühl!" said Isy, shepherding them to the door.

When they were on the underground, she explained that Gummy Bear and Tannhäuser would be accompanying Josepha to the mill.

"Amanda and I can't be late for our clients, so the boys will go with you," she told Josepha. "They're from 7b as well. When you get to Brinkenbühl, you'll be looked after by a lovely old lady. By the way, none of them know who you are!"

Isy had made three telephone calls that morning: the first to Mrs von Leinungen, the second to Gummy Bear, and the third to Tannhäuser. It was hard to believe that they had swallowed her story. Even Isy had thought it was pretty far-fetched, but she had convinced them that truth could be stranger than fiction.

"Isy told them that your name was Harissa and that you've gone into hiding because your parents want to fly you to Damascus to marry a bald-headed businessman," explained Amanda. She didn't mention the fact that Isy had **pledged** a couple of football scarves in return for their classmates' help. It was typical of Isy, who was hopeless at knitting, to rely on her good-natured friend.

Josepha smiled. "Cool! Who's Tannhäuser?"

"Reginald Häuser. He loves Wagner and he speaks like Udo Lindenberg. He's the smartest

---

to pledge – *(hier)* versprechen

pupil in our class. Gummy Bear's brain is the size of a cherry tomato."

"Opposites attract, I guess."

"Like Janho and you, I suppose." Isy wished she hadn't said anything when Josepha smiled mysteriously from behind her sunglasses.

"That's a little too personal," she said, acting like a movie star who was tired of dealing with **prying** reporters.

The train stopped and neither Amanda nor Josepha had time to notice Isy's embarrassment. She couldn't believe that they were risking everything for a **stuck-up** madam who gave herself **airs and graces**. She was so **incensed** with Josepha that she stumbled out of the train, almost falling onto the platform. To think that Janho was attracted to such an ungrateful cow!

Isy was still fuming long after Reginald and Hagen had escorted Josepha to Brinkenbühl. She felt moody and bad-tempered while she and Amanda rushed through their tasks. There was even less time than usual because they were meeting Gummy Bear and Tannhäuser at the Bornsteins' apartment in the afternoon. Isy knew that the boys would want to hear the full story, but she had no desire to tell them everything. The question was, how much did they need to know?

---

to pry – neugierig sein; stuck-up – hochnäsig;
to give oneself airs and graces – vornehm tun;
incensed – aufgebracht

If it were up to her, she wouldn't have involved them in the first place. They were bound to force their way in on the act. She was tempted to **fob them off** with another story, but Amanda had made her promise not to tackle the criminal on her own. She wondered whether her friend had realized that the boys would expect a share of the reward …

It was their last visit to Wolodja's apartment. She mopped up the puddles while Amanda chatted on her mobile upstairs.

"Do we have to empty Lullula arborea's mailbox?" she asked Isy when she was finally off the phone.

"Our woodlark is back in Berlin – thank goodness!"

Isy carried the bucket of dirty water into the bathroom and poured it down the toilet. She washed her hands, dried them carefully and took a look in the mirror. Her mother was right: she looked tired. Wolodja was still cowering under the sofa. Isy shot him a friendly glance. "It's all right, old boy, your mistress will be home tomorrow," she said, bidding him farewell.

They went to see Gottfried, then finished their duties with a trip to Otti and Lotti's.

Tearing off their wigs, they arrived at Amanda's apartment with only minutes to spare. As usual, her parents weren't home. Her dad worked long

---

to fob s.o. off – jmdn. abspeisen

hours at the office and her mum was always shopping or riding in Grunewald.

"Why do you need a six-room apartment?" asked Isy, making herself comfortable on Amanda's blue **inflatable** chair. "Your parents are never here!"

Her friend grinned. "You should hear my mum complaining about the miserly size of apartments in East Berlin. She'd rather live in a Cluedo mansion!"

Isy put up her feet and listened to a Madonna CD.

"Isn't it great? An apartment where we can finally relax without watering the plants, talking to the goldfish, feeding the birds or stroking the cats!" She yawned contentedly.

"We've still got Aeschylus," said Amanda, watering the cactus lovingly.

Aeschylus could be extremely useful at times. Amanda took him everywhere with her – including on holiday.

"I miss Alfredo," said Isy sadly.

"I don't," said her friend.

The doorbell rang. Hagen Golz, otherwise known as Gummy Bear, and Reginald Häuser, aka Tannhäuser, were standing on the doorstep. They had accompanied 'Harissa' as far as Brinkenbühl and delivered her into the care of Mrs von Leinungen who had been waiting at the bus stop as promised.

---

inflatable – aufblasbar

"The **bartered bride** sends her regards," **drawled** Tannhäuser, casting himself onto Amanda's bed. Gummy Bear studied the poster of Prince William.

"Do you mean Harissa?" asked Amanda.

"It's probably an opera by Wagner," guessed Isy.

"It's by Smetana, actually. If it were by Wagner, I'd be familiar with the plot!" Tannhäuser said sharply.

"Operas are boring," objected Gummy Bear, sitting down at Amanda's computer and logging himself in. "Let's put it another way. What's the definition of stupid?"

Tannhäuser put up his hand and supplied the answer. "Amanda Bornstein and Isolde Schütze!"

Amanda frowned and glanced at Isy. "I think our guests would like to leave," she said frostily.

Gummy Bear didn't seem to notice her displeasure. The cursor darted over Amanda's files.

"Hands off! What are you doing in my documents?" demanded Amanda.

"Looking for your love letters!"

"Good luck to you! I keep them on my mobile!"

"OK, enough fooling around," growled Gummy Bear, suddenly serious. "Do you think we're idiots or something?"

Isy knew at once that the boys had guessed the truth. It wasn't exactly surprising.

"I don't know why you're being so aggressive,"

---

the bartered bride – die verkaufte Braut *(Oper von Smetana)*;
to drawl – gedehnt sprechen

said Amanda. "You'll get your scarves like Isy promised. Would you like a can of coke?"

"It's not coke that we're after," laughed Gummy Bear. "We want fifty per cent!"

"Fifty per cent? Fifty per cent of what?" enquired Amanda, playing dumb.

"What do you think Reggi? Are these the hardened criminals who kidnapped Josepha?"

"How dare you?" said Amanda, practically gasping with indignation. "We rescued Josepha. We saved her from danger."

"So you admit it, do you?" asked Tannhäuser triumphantly.

Amanda's eyes widened in horror as she realized what she'd said, but Isy had decided to come clean. "We found her by chance."

"Then why are you hiding her in Brinkenbühl? Why not take her back to her parents and pocket the reward?"

"Because we wanted to share it with you," hissed Amanda.

"Actually, we wanted to make sure that the criminal didn't **get off scot-free**," explained her friend. "He pretended to be a famous movie director by the name of Wolfram B. Braun, but his real name is Lothar Loll. I knew there was something fishy about him as soon as I met him. Poor Amanda thought he was going to launch her movie career."

"You mean you've actually met him?" chorused Tannhäuser and Gummy Bear in **awe**.

---

to get off scot-free – unbestraft davonkommen; awe – Ehrfurcht

"Sure. We didn't realize it was him. He signed up for our holiday service."

The boys listened in **rapt** suspense while Isy told them what had happened. She included every single detail – except of course the sorry tale of Amanda's debtor and her planned career as a forger.

"You really are calamity queens!" muttered Gummy Bear, impressed. Isy realized that the boys had stopped thinking about the money and were interested in the case. Their eyes were shining with excitement and they were practically falling over themselves in their eagerness to help. The first challenge was to work out Lothar Loll's real profession. What sort of job would give him access to empty homes?

"He could be an **estate agent**," proposed Amanda.

"Or a handyman," growled Gummy Bear.

"I reckon he's a **house clearance** specialist," said Tannhäuser.

"A house-clearance specialist?" echoed Isy, looking up from her notes. "What's that?"

"Someone who clears out empty homes and gets rid of the furniture. People hire them when someone dies and there aren't any relatives to go through their possessions. You can hire a house-clearance agency if you're moving abroad."

"You might be onto something," muttered Isy,

---

rapt – hingerissen;
estate agent – Häusermakler;
house clearance – Entrümpelung

chewing on her pen. "So you could hire a house-clearance specialist if you inherited a house?"

"Absolutely."

Isy leant back with a satisfied expression on her face. "That's it then. Lothar Loll works in house-clearance. He has access to plenty of empty apartments because people hire him to **dispose of** their furniture. He was able to hide Josepha, but he had to make sure that she wouldn't stray outside. The little idiot did exactly as he told her because he promised her a new identity and some plastic surgery."

"Mrs Boskov must have hired him when she inherited the house from her aunt. That's how he knew Josepha's family," deduced Amanda. "But I don't see why she would have told him about the 500,000 euros."

"Maybe she didn't," said Tannhäuser. "Maybe he was the one who realized the true value of the house. He'd know all about antique furniture, rare paintings and the like."

"Either way, he found out about her fortune, and he decided to **rip her off** ." Isy's cheeks were glowing with excitement. The scriptwriters for 'Tatort' would kill for a story like this!

"He tricked Josepha into trusting him and set up the supposed kidnapping in order to trick Mrs Boskov into paying him the money. And then he hired us to deliver bread rolls to the miss-

---

to dispose of – loswerden;
to rip s.o. off – jmdn. übervorteilen

ing Josepha until the end of the month. What a cheek!"

"We'll hide out in the apartment and wait for him," said Gummy Bear. "We should probably take a can of pepper gas with us. Do you have a key?"

Amanda nodded. "According to Josepha, Lothar Loll will be returning to the apartment at four o'clock on Halloween."

"In that case, we need to arrive by one thirty at the latest. We ought to allow ourselves plenty of time to hide."

"What if he doesn't come? What if he smells a rat?" asked Tannhäuser, trying to identify potential problems. He was right to be cautious, but they decided to risk it anyway.

Amanda and Tannhäuser were the only ones with mobile phones. They swapped numbers so they could contact each other in an emergency. The codeword was 'Harissa'.

They chatted for a while, then Amanda sent the boys packing. She was looking forward to a six-course celebratory dinner to mark the end of her cookery course. While the Spice Girls sang 'Viva forever' in the background, she put on her trendiest black T-shirt and applied some shiny pink eye shadow.

"I hope your cookery course was worth it," remarked Isy as she waved the smoke out of the window and put the empty coke cans in the bin. "Are you going to cook an Italian masterpiece for Mr Rimpau?"

"I was thinking more along the lines of something Chinese: minced meat and Shanghai **bean-thread noodles**. The Chinese call it 'ants climbing a tree'."

"Ugh! You can't be serious! Why don't you make it for Otti and Lotti instead?"

"Don't worry, it's made with pork, not ants."

"I'd rather not risk it. Why not settle for pumpkin pie instead? The programme's tomorrow, isn't it?"

A wail went up from the bathroom.

"My pumpkin's gone missing! I think I've lost it!"

— 22 —

The pumpkin had gone missing and neither Isy nor Amanda could figure out how.

It was the only topic of conversation that morning. For the first time in ages, they had started the weekend with a relaxed family breakfast before leaving their respective apartments in order to devote themselves to the few remaining plants, animals and mailboxes whose owners were still away.

"I bet it's at Otti and Lotti's!" said Isy.

"It can't be! I know for a fact that I didn't take it with me to Mrs von Leinungen's apartment."

"In that case it's at Gottfried's," declared Isy. "It's hardly surprising that we don't know where you left it. I can hardly remember all the places we've been."

---

bean-thread noodles – Glasnudeln

They visited the **unflappable** goldfish in Karlshorst but Amanda's precious pumpkin wasn't there.

"Did we take it to Wolodja's?" wondered Isy.

Amanda shook her head. "That was pumpkin number two. We lost it on the underground, remember?"

"That's right. And pumpkin three came from a supermarket. But where did we take it after that?"

"To apartment 1101!" came the triumphant reply from Amanda. "We thought we were going to Wolfram B. Braun's grandmother. We didn't know that Josepha was devouring our bread rolls!"

"You're right," said Isy, relieved. "And from there we went to Pioschleck's penthouse. We must have left it there!"

Luckily for them, Pio's apartment was next on the list.

They fed Gottfried and changed his water, then made their way back to the inner city, pushing their way through the slow-moving crowds. Every Saturday families descended in their **droves** on central Berlin to go shopping.

They were only a few paces from Pio's trendy apartment block when Amanda clutched her friend's arm. A pale-faced girl was looking through the window of an expensive boutique. Isy stared as the girl turned and walked towards them. Wasn't Jennifer Niemann supposed to be sunning herself

---

unflappable – nicht aus der Ruhe zu bringen;
drove – *(hier)* Schar

in the Dominican Republic? Why hadn't she got a tan? Isy tried not to laugh. Jennifer had a reputation for telling tall stories. Everyone in 7b was wise to her **fibs**.

"Keep calm," she whispered. "We're in disguise, remember."

Jennifer Niemann showed no sign of recognizing them. Just as they were drawing level, Amanda issued a muttered warning: "You can't hide the truth forever, Jennifer."

Jennifer Niemann froze and stared at them in horror. They darted into Pio's apartment block and collapsed with laughter. Unlike last time, they didn't have the added challenge of **sneaking** a **swaddled** Josepha past reception. There was no sign of the porter anywhere. The telephone behind the desk kept ringing and ringing.

"It reminds me of New York," said Amanda, fishing three letters and a **wad** of junk mail out of Pio's tray. "Except a New York apartment block would have a security guard on the gates."

"Does Pio have a parking space?"

"There's even an underground car park. This place has everything!" declared Amanda. They stepped into the elevator, which played music at them while they ascended to Pio's floor. Isy stopped to take an admiring look at the handsome terracot-

---

fib – kleine (Not-)Lüge;
to sneak in – *(hier)* s. hineinschmuggeln;
swaddled – eingehüllt;
wad – dicker Stapel

ta vase outside his door. Amanda pointed to the neighbour's nameplate and laughed.

"Dr Alois Kirschpubs! What a ridiculous name!" exclaimed Isy.

They went into the apartment. What it lacked in size, it made up for in style. Isy was particularly impressed by the American-style kitchen of **sumptuous** marble and shiny wood. She examined the room more closely. There was a magnificent view of Berlin from the windows, and the furniture and appliances were made of trendy leather, chrome and glass. The effect was very cool, but Isy couldn't help thinking that something was missing.

"You'd think he'd have more recipe books."

"He keeps them at his main house. Cooking can be quite stressful you know," explained Amanda, who was speaking from experience. "He tends to go to restaurants when he's staying in Berlin."

"How do you know?"

"His housekeeper told me. She told me to be discreet. Staff aren't supposed to gossip about their famous employers."

She was interrupted by her mobile phone. Depositing Pio's mail on his imposing antique bureau, she rushed into the hall to rummage through her jacket pockets and answer her phone. Isy heard her chatting brightly and suspected that it was Ruky. Maybe he was finally going to pay off his debt to the **charitable** Bumblebee. Isy knew that Amanda occasionally exchanged texts and faxes with the

---

sumptuous – kostbar, prächtig; charitable – mildtätig

handsome half-Cuban from Altgrünheide, but she couldn't understand what had prompted Amanda to part with her savings. It seemed to Isy that her friend **had a crush on** Ruky. In fact, Amanda had probably fancied him from the start – in spite of his relationship with fair-haired Doreen, the baker's daughter. She wished that her friend had **confided in** her earlier. If she, Isolde Schütze, had loaned her savings to Ruky, she would have told Amanda straightaway. As a punishment, she decided not to tell Amanda that she had a thing for Janho von Leinungen. The truth was, she daydreamed about him every day.

Just then Amanda reappeared in the lounge.

"It was only Tannhäuser."

"What did he want?" enquired Isy suspiciously.

"An update, that's all. He was full of his own importance. I bet they're after the reward."

Ashamed of herself for misjudging her friend, Isy helped Amanda hunt for the missing vegetable. Amanda gave a full description of pumpkin number three.

"It had a little **protuberance** on one side. It looked almost like an ear."

It soon became apparent that they were wasting their time. There was no trace of a pumpkin – with or without an ear. **Dejected**, Amanda plonked herself down on a chair.

---

to have a crush on s.o. – in jmdn. vernarrt sein;
to confide in s.o. – sich jmdm. anvertrauen;
protuberance – Höcker; dejected – niedergeschlagen

"There's another possibility, you know," her friend ventured cautiously. "What if we didn't take the pumpkin to Pioschleck's? What if we were so shocked at finding Josepha that we…"

Amanda stared at her, aghast. She didn't need Isy to explain any further. Pumpkin number three had been abandoned in Lothar Loll's living room.

"We followed Josepha into the apartment, and you took a seat at the desk. After a while I heard a thud. Do you think you might have dropped it?"

"Oh gosh," said Amanda. "I bet it rolled under the desk. I wasn't thinking straight. You're not mad at me, are you, Isy?"

"Of course not! Do you think we should go back and get it?"

"No way!" said Amanda, jumping up in horror and grabbing the keys. "What if he catches us? I'd rather buy a new one instead."

The first supermarket had run out of pumpkins and so had the second. "It's Halloween next week," explained the cashier. "We haven't got a single pumpkin left!"

They had just given up and were leaving the shop when three police cars sped down the street, blue lights flashing. Amanda thought she spotted Detective Rose in the back of one of the cars. The prickly policeman had a habit of **popping up** everywhere.

Isy wondered whether Amanda was mistaken. "It's one thing talking to a bunch of schoolkids, but

---

to pop up – auftauchen

I can't see him tackling a violent criminal." She knew how detectives were supposed to act. Some made a bull-like impression, others were gentlemanly, and a few pretended to be **twits**. The latter were particularly dangerous. Detective Rose didn't fit any of those categories. He was different. He stood out because of his ordinariness. She didn't expect Amanda to notice a thing like that.

But Professor Pioschleck's programme was due to start in an hour and they didn't have a pumpkin. Amanda was so **downcast** that Isy felt miserable as well.

"Tell you what," she said comfortingly. "Why don't you watch the programme and take notes? We'll buy a pumpkin later, and you can try the recipe on Mr Rimpau and me. OK?"

Amanda cheered up immediately. She was dying to try her hand at pumpkin pie, but Isy was right: she could wait for a few more days. In a **fit** of enthusiasm, she asked her friend to watch the programme as well.

Her invitation was rejected **outright**. "I never watch cookery programmes!"

"Can't you make an exception?"

"No," said Isy, who was looking forward to getting back to her crime novel.

"In that case, don't expect me to watch your bor-

---

twit – Blödmann;
downcast – niedergeschlagen;
fit – Anfall;
outright – gänzlich

ing crime shows." Disappointed, Amanda headed home on her own and sat down in front of the television with a salami sandwich and a packet of tortillas. Pio's programmes always made her hungry.

She was about to take her first bite when the doorbell rang. It was probably someone wanting to talk to her mother, who was riding Amado in Grunewald. Annoyed at the interruption, she marched down the hall and opened the door.

"Has it started already?" gasped Isy, barging past her into the lounge.

"I thought you didn't like cookery shows?" exclaimed Amanda.

"I decided to make an exception." Grinning, Isy collapsed onto the white sofa and took a bite of Amanda's sandwich.

The **opening credits** came up on the screen, accompanied by the theme tune. The camera **panned** to the bright yellow kitchen, and Pioschleck appeared in the frame. The blue-eyed professor smiled at the audience and introduced his guest, a young actress who was starring in a new TV series. She would be demonstrating how to make her mother's specialty salad.

As promised, the professor produced a large orange pumpkin, which he chopped into pieces while Amanda noted down the ingredients from the list on the screen.

"Fantastic," she murmured appreciatively. "Plen-

---

opening credits – Vorspann;
to pan – schwenken

ty of sugar and cinnamon – you'll love this one, Isy."

She watched with rapt attention as Pio removed a kilo of baked pumpkin from the oven and left it on the side to cool. A moment later, his powerful hands were **kneading** a ball of pastry while he explained to the audience that the pie was based on an American recipe

Amanda was **intent on jotting down** his every word, but Isy's mind kept wandering. She thought of the thrilling crime novel that she had abandoned at home.

"How was your celebratory meal?"

"Delicious!" said Amanda, licking her lips. "I ate so much I almost burst. Everyone else paid up for the rest of the course. I told the chef that I'd forgotten my wallet and that I'd give him the cash on Monday."

"We'll have the money by then. Tomorrow is payday!"

Professor Pioschleck was in the process of scraping the baked pumpkin into a **blender**. He added eggs, sugar and sour cream to the bright orange puree. Meanwhile, the young actress was **grating** carrots and twittering about rolls and roles of the edible and theatrical variety. Then Pio rolled out

---

to knead – kneten;
to be intent on – sich konzentrieren auf;
to jot down – schnell notieren;
blender – Pürieraufsatz einer Küchenmaschine;
to grate – reiben

the pastry and lined the base and sides of a pre-greased tin. He poured the pumpkin puree on top and added a generous sprinkling of grated **lemon zest** and cinnamon. Finally he placed the tin in a pre-heated oven and – as if by magic – produced a piping hot pumpkin pie from the upper shelf. He used the same trick at the end of every show.

For a moment they could practically smell the lovely golden crust and the tantalizing aroma of melted butter and cinnamon.

"He's amazing, isn't he?" whispered Amanda, waiting for Isy to agree.

Isy nodded dutifully. "He's an excellent chef. Is the programme over or is there a **twist**?"

"It's a cookery programme, not a crime show! Of course it's over!"

At that moment the live audience started whispering excitedly. The camera panned to the left where two men were hurrying towards the yellow kitchen. One of them looked strangely familiar.

"It's Detective Rose!" gasped Amanda, shocked. "What's he doing in Pio's kitchen?"

"Maybe he wants an autograph?" chuckled Isy.

Suddenly the sound was cut. The startled professor's lips were moving, but the words weren't audible. It was like watching a silent movie. The detective with the flowery name said something, then **whipped out** a metal gadget from his pocket.

---

lemon zest – Zitronenschale;
twist – *(hier)* unerwartete Wendung;
to whip out – schnell hervorholen

Isy and Amanda huddled together on the sofa and watched in horrified silence as the **handcuffs** closed on Professor Pio's wrists.

– 23 –

"**Pumpkin Crime**!" screamed the Sunday papers. "Professor Pioschleck arrested!"

Isy and Amanda stared aghast at the billboards at the railway kiosk. Earlier that morning they had read the first reports over breakfast, but the latest headlines said exactly the same.

The **task force** in charge of the Boskov investigation had received an anonymous **tip-off** about a penthouse in central Berlin. The raid on Professor Pioschleck's apartment had taken place at noon on Saturday, and the porter on duty had been present.

The forensic investigators had been intending to **scour** the penthouse for DNA evidence, but a blue-and-yellow friendship bracelet had been discovered in the shower. Mrs Boskov had subsequently confirmed that it belonged to her daughter.

Less than an hour later, Detective Rose, known throughout the police force as a prickly character, had raced to the television studios and arrested Professor Pioschleck, who was filming an episode

---

handcuffs – Handschellen;
task force – Sonderkommando;
tip-off – Hinweis;
to scour – durchkämmen

about pumpkin pie. Protesting his innocence, the TV chef had stated that he hadn't set foot in his Berlin apartment for the past three weeks. He was still being questioned. A search was underway for his housekeeper, who was supposedly on holiday in the Netherlands.

"Everyone will think he did it," said Amanda, her voice trembling with rage.

"Call Reginald!" said Isy. "Codeword 'Harissa'! It's an emergency. Tell him to meet us at your place this afternoon – assuming that your parents won't be in."

"I think they've gone for coffee with some friends," mumbled Amanda, rummaging in her pockets for her mobile. "What did I tell you about hiding Josepha in Pio's apartment? I knew it was a bad idea!" She glared at Isy out of the corner of her eye while she waited for Tannhäuser to answer. "I could tell from the start that Josepha would be trouble. She broke her word about smoking in the apartment, she left her bracelet in the shower, and now Pio is in prison. Isy, we've got to help him!"

Isy bowed her head **sheepishly**, knowing that Amanda was right. It was awful to think that an innocent man had been arrested because of their mistake. She felt guilty – but more than anything, she felt annoyed. It didn't make sense. Why had the police suspected Pio? Amanda was obviously wondering the same.

---

sheepish – betreten, schüchtern

"Who tipped them off?" she asked angrily as soon as Tannhäuser had rung off.

"The porter!" said Isy.

"The porter? Don't be ridiculous! Josepha was wearing a disguise." Amanda shook her **fake** blonde curls. "If you ask me, it can only have been one person, and I'm going to **give him a piece of my mind**."

"What about collecting our wages?"

"Start without me. I'll meet you at Otti and Lotti's."

"Where are you going?" shouted Isy, but Amanda was already charging out of the station. She swept through the streets like a hurricane, puffing in the chilly morning air. At last she came to a halt in front of a tower block. She was **incandescent** with rage.

Her failure to protect the professor made her doubly determined to **exact** her **revenge**. Unbeknown to anyone, including Isy, Amanda sometimes felt like Lara Croft. She was usually too lethargic to play the action heroine, but at last her moment had come.

She ran on, throwing her weight against the door, sprinting past the graffiti in the entrance hall and charging up three flights of stairs. A collection

---

fake – falsch;
to give s.o. a piece of one's mind – jmdm. ordentlich die Meinung sagen;
incandescent – glühend;
to exact revenge – Rache erzwingen

of shoes in different sizes led her to the appropriate door.

Two weeks ago, she and Isy had stopped here to drop off Alfredo on their way to Brinkenbühl mill. They had been welcomed by the youngest member of the family, who had taken one look at their costumes and slammed the door.

"It's you again," said the little girl in surprise, peering through a crack in the battered door.

Amanda finally stopped pressing the doorbell. "Can I come in this time?" she asked, slipping her hand through the crack and ruffling the youngster's hair.

Striding through the apartment, she traced the tantalizing smell of bacon, eggs and coffee to a table in the living room where the family was eating breakfast together.

To her surprise, no one turned round when she entered the room. Everyone was staring intently at the television. The volume was painfully loud. The eldest boy stopped buttering his toast and looked round in confusion when she tapped his shoulder.

"What are you doing here?"

"You weren't expecting me, huh?" said Amanda grimly. "Here's a present from Pioschleck!"

She picked up his plate and threw the sloppy, fat-streaked mass of **scrambled eggs** into Gummy Bear's face.

---

scrambled eggs – Rührei

— 24 —

Revenge is a *dish best served cold,* thought Isy, who usually switched off when grown-ups peppered their conversation with proverbs. But in this case her grandma's favourite saying was proving **apt**.

Admittedly, it didn't specifically mention scrambled eggs, but it was perfect in every other respect. Luckily for Amanda, her act of **vengeance** hadn't caused any lasting harm. It was particularly fortunate, given the injustice of the accusation. Hagen Golz knew nothing of Pioschleck's apartment. He and Tannhäuser had escorted Josepha to Brinkenbühl. If either of them had wanted to tip off the police, they would have sent them to the Cluedo mansion where the missing girl was in hiding, protected by the unsuspecting Mrs von Leinungen. They knew Josepha's **whereabouts**, so why would they send the police somewhere else?

No, Gummy Bear hadn't made the anonymous phone call, although Amanda was **loath** to believe it. "Someone tipped them off," she said angrily. "Who else could it have been?" It was upsetting to learn that Lara Croft's instincts had been wrong.

"I wish I knew," sighed Isy. Anonymous callers were notoriously difficult to trace – even for the

---

apt – treffend;
vengeance – Rache;
whereabouts – zeitweiliger Aufenthaltsort;
to be loath to do s.th. – etwas ungern tun

police. Maybe they would never find out who had **blabbed** about Pio's apartment. The real mystery was how the caller had spotted the missing girl.

Josepha couldn't possibly have ventured outside the penthouse because she didn't have a key. Whoever had seen her, had spotted her *inside* the apartment, which meant the culprit was either psychic or had the ability to see through walls.

The Boskov saga was Isy's toughest case yet. She kept finding new pieces of the jigsaw, but the puzzle just seemed to grow.

Isy had met Amanda at Otti and Lotti's at ten. They had waited for the cats to **polish off** their Cantonese seafood, then made their way to Max's place. Isy could feel her wallet in her jacket pocket. It was bulging with hard-earned cash. "Look, we're rich," she had told Amanda as they were leaving Mrs von Leinungen's apartment.

Strictly speaking, the money belonged to Amanda – or to the Italian chef whom she had promised to pay on Monday. So far they had earned more than expected – thanks to some generous tips in recognition of their work. Even the **dour**-faced Mrs Ober-Lippe had donated an extra ten euros. But the thought of the money wasn't enough to lift Amanda's mood.

Isy had tried to cheer her up. "Come on, Mandi,

---

to blab – sich verplappern;
to polish off – verputzen;
dour – streng

Pio will be able to prove that he hasn't been near his apartment. He'll be out of prison in no time."

"The police want to question his housekeeper. She'll tell them it was us!"

"She'll point the finger at a couple of holiday angels – but she won't know who we are! Stop worrying and think about our cash!"

"It's great to have the money, but what about Pio? Think of what he must be going through because of us!"

"We'll apologize later, I promise. Just imagine the headlines when we explain what really happened. *Josepha Saved by Pio's Penthouse*! *Abductor* ***Foiled*** *by TV Chef*! He'll be grateful for the publicity!"

Amanda **perked up** slightly. "In that case, we'd better hurry. People will spread the most dreadful rumours until we clear his name."

Just as she had predicted, the professor's arrest was the talk of the town. Isy and Amanda heard his name everywhere – among the appetizing smell of curried sausage at the hot dog stand; in the murmured conversations of passers-by; and in the passengers' small-talk on the bus. Amanda felt like sticking her fingers in her ears.

"It's scandalous," muttered a female passenger. "He's such a talented chef and he always seems so charming. I watch his programme every week. And to think he abducted that girl!" She sounded shocked and bewildered.

---

to foil – vereiteln; to perk up – sich wieder erholen

"I heard that he needs the money," replied her neighbour **spitefully**.

"What nonsense!" retorted a third woman, interrupting their conversation. "Professor Pioschleck is a gentleman. Someone knew that his penthouse was empty and shamelessly abused his trust!"

"How right you are!" exclaimed Amanda at the top of her voice. The other passengers swivelled round and stared. "Some people will be left with **egg on their faces**, just you wait and see!"

She was prevented from explaining more fully because the bus had pulled up at their stop.

Isy was silently praying that Max wouldn't offer Amanda another tumbler of red wine. She needn't have worried. There was no sign of the student – with or without his red wine. No one answered the door.

"We specifically told him that we'd be collecting our money," grumbled Amanda, while Isy put her ear to the door. The apartment was quiet.

She wondered whether they should let themselves in. They were in possession of a key – but maybe they didn't have the authority to use it. She decided to take a more subtle approach.

"Gottfried will be waiting for us," she said loudly. "Come on, Amanda, let's go!" Grabbing her startled friend, she hurried in the direction of the upstairs landing. They looked down just in time to

---

spiteful – boshaft;

to have egg on one's face – blamiert dastehen

see a mop of dark curls **poking** out of the door. It was like watching a **woodpecker** peering out of a tree trunk.

"Hey Max!" called Isy. "We thought you were out!"

Max glanced up in surprise. "I didn't see you up there! Someone rang the doorbell, but I thought it was a bunch of kids."

Amanda stared at him suspiciously. "You said we could collect our money today!"

"You should have let yourselves in," he answered **breezily**. He ushered them into his apartment as if the door had been open all the time.

As usual, they had to fight their way through the muddle of books, magazines and abandoned black socks. Max unscrewed a bottle of alcohol.

"I thought I'd thank my charming little angels with a glass of premium Finnish vodka. Unless you'd prefer a joint?"

"Vodka for me, thanks," said Amanda uncertainly, but Isy butted in. "We'd rather have our money. The bill comes to thirty euros. I'm afraid we're in a rush."

"What about the student discount?"

"It's already included."

Max frowned and scratched his head.

Isy knew at once that he had no intention of paying. No wonder he hadn't wanted to open the door!

---

to poke – hervorstechen;
woodpecker – Specht;
breezy – flott

Her thoughts were distracted by the small TV set that was **perched** on the bookcase. Max had been watching a crime movie. A man was sitting by a window, peering through his camera into someone's apartment.

"Classic Hitchcock," said Max. "It's his best film."

"Pardon me," spluttered Amanda, "but we **traipsed** across Berlin every single day to feed your darling Leila. Forty euros is our standard rate. We made an exception for you!"

"It's still a lot of money for a student!"

"It's a lot of money for two schoolgirls as well!"

"Schoolgirls?" echoed Max, taken aback. "I thought you said you were students?"

That's that, then, thought Isy sadly. Amanda had **scuppered** any hope of recovering the money by revealing the truth about their age.

Her friend seemed to realize her mistake. Jumping off her chair as if she'd been bitten by a tarantula, she hurried to the tortoise's enclosure. "OK, Max, here's the deal: either you **cough up**, or Leila comes with us." She plunged her hand into the terrarium, then stopped suddenly. Her arm dangled limply by her side. "Where is she?"

"In the fridge."

"What?!" gasped Isy and Amanda, horrified.

---

to perch – hocken;
to traipse – latschen;
to scupper – zuschanden machen;
cough up – blechen

"I put her in the fridge. Hibernation lasts from the end of October to the end of February. It's what the vet recommends." Max **stubbed out** his cigarette. "I might be rubbish with money, but I'd never hurt an animal. Leila is my best friend!"

"Fine," said Amanda, unmoved. "When are you going to get us the money?"

There was an awkward pause while Amanda tried to make eye contact with her friend.

But Isy was staring raptly at the television on the bookcase. The man with the camera was watching while someone committed a murder in the other flat. Why didn't he rush over and stop the killer?

"He's in a wheelchair," explained Max. "I can lend you the tape if you like."

Isy stared at him blankly. "Er, sorry, I've just remembered something. Come on, Amanda, I've had an idea!"

"What about our money?" asked Amanda as Isy dragged her away. "Why the hurry?"

"The window!"

"Max's window?"

"The window in the film! We've got to go back to the penthouse!"

"I thought we were going to Gottfried's."

"We'll go there later."

"But it's Sunday lunch. Mum told me to be punctual."

"So did mine. But I thought you wanted to know who blabbed about Josepha!"

---

to stub out – ausdrücken

– 25 –

Of course Amanda wanted to know who had blabbed about Josepha! Grumbling under her breath about Max and the money, she followed Isy to the nearest underground station and they made their way back to Pio's apartment. They were still some distance away when they noticed the pack of photographers camped on the pavement. Jo Scribbler and his snap-happy photographer were waiting outside the lobby as well.

Isy stopped and froze. "We'll never get through," she said **despondently**, cursing herself for not anticipating the crowds of journalists.

This time it was Amanda who came up with the solution. She made straight for a nearby car park and hurried to a staircase that led into another car park; the car park in the basement of Pio's block! Two figures in green uniforms were stationed at the entrance. Isy and Amanda crouched behind a Mercedes van until the policemen were looking the other way. They darted through a steel door at the far end of the car park and ran through a **maze** of white corridors. At last they came to an elevator.

"Thank goodness," gasped Amanda, pressing the button for the eleventh floor.

Her relief was short-lived. The doors opened on the ground floor and a policeman peered inside.

---

despondent – niedergeschlagen;
maze – Irrgarten

"I'm afraid you'll have to tell me what you're doing here."

"We're visiting Dr Alois Kirschpubs," said Amanda without hesitating. She whipped out Professor Pio's keys for the policeman to see.

Isy was impressed by her friend's **ingenuity**. It was lucky that Professor Pio's neighbour had such an unusual name.

"Is it a social call?"

"We're his holiday angels. We look after his plants."

"I see," said the policeman, glancing at their blonde wigs and blue glasses. "Can I see some ID?"

They stared at him, aghast.

"It's just a formality. We're trying to keep out the reporters – we caught a few of them sneaking through the lobby in disguise."

Isy could see that Amanda was panicking.

"Stuck at home with the rubber plant? Holiday cancelled because of cat & co.? We can solve your problems," said Isy rattling off the advert from memory. *"The helpful staff at* Making Holidays Happen *will take care of your loved ones while you go away. Call now and book your holiday angel."* She paused and smiled. "Come to think of it, you probably know our favourite client. You're acquainted with Detective Rose, aren't you? He trusts us implicitly."

The young officer was so surprised that two round **dimples** appeared on his cheeks.

---

ingenuity – Erfindungsgabe; dimple – Grübchen

"Detective Rose? He's always telling us that he never has time for a holiday!" He winked at them **roguishly**. "It's good to know the boss is human! Sorry for bothering you." He sent the elevator on its way.

"Gosh, that was close," gasped Amanda. Relieved, they continued to the eleventh storey, but Pio's apartment was sealed off by yards of yellow tape.

"Do you see that? They'll never let us in."

"That's not why we're here," said Isy, striding down the corridor. Her fingers **fumbled** with the **catch** of the arched window. She leaned over the white windowsill and surveyed the neighbouring buildings. It didn't take long to work out which building she was after: it was the tower block diagonally opposite the penthouse. More specifically, it was the apartment on the top storey. From the balcony, someone with binoculars would be able to see straight into Pio's kitchen!

"Aren't you going to tell me what's going on?" asked Amanda impatiently. Her stomach was rumbling and it was time for Sunday lunch.

But Isy was on the move again. "Just five more minutes," she promised, hurrying back to the elevator.

They left via the lobby and pushed their way through the crowd of reporters. Isy observed Jo

---

roguish – schelmisch;
to fumble – herumfummeln;
catch – *(hier)* Riegel

Scribbler out of the corner of her eye. He looked up sharply and took a step towards her, but she darted across the road and dived into an apartment block, with Amanda struggling to keep up. Neither spoke as they waited for the elevator to reach the top floor. Isy marched up to an apartment that smelt of roast meat and red cabbage. She rang the doorbell, knowing that she needed to concoct a convincing story to be invited inside.

"Congratulations!" she said to the silver-haired woman who was peering at them in astonishment through her glasses. "We're your lucky angels! Do you mind if we come inside?" Pushing past the woman, she sped into the front room where a bald man was eating his roast. He stood up in surprise.

"Don't let me spoil your meal," said Isy politely as she strode to the window and peeked through the lace curtains. Judging by the lack of balcony, she had picked the wrong apartment.

"I think we've won something, Hermann," said the woman to her husband. Amanda was staring hungrily at the food on their plates. "They're our lucky angels."

The elderly couple turned to Isy in expectation. She tried to look apologetic.

"Oh, I'm really sorry, but we must have made a mistake. This is the wrong apartment. The prize winner lives next-door."

"Did you see what they were eating? Roast beef and red cabbage with raisins! It looked delicious," said Amanda enviously. Isy rang the neighbour's doorbell.

This time it was answered by the hoarse bark of an ageing dog. There was no sign of its owner.

Isy suspected that someone was looking at them through the spy hole. She read the name shield: 'Grigoleit'. Amanda put her nose to the door. "Stuffed peppers," she said hungrily.

"Is anyone home?" called Isy. She gave a gentle knock. "Please, it's important."

The dog barked louder than ever, and finally a thin **reedy** voice piped up. "Who's there?"

"It's a surprise!" said Isy brightly.

The door opened a little, and a woman stared at Isy with dark suspicious eyes. "I don't want anything to do with the police."

"We're not policewomen, Mrs Grigoleit."

"I don't want anything to do with the papers."

"We're not journalists, either. We're your lucky angels! You've won a prize!"

The mention of a prize worked wonders. The door opened and Mrs Grigoleit became more communicative.

"Do you mean the lottery? I never buy tickets."

"It's a ... special Sunday competition. We picked your name from thousands of others in the phone book. Congratulations!"

The elderly lady looked excited and ushered them in. She **padded** into the living room in her green silk slippers, with her ancient cocker spaniel at her heels. The room was the same size and shape

---

reedy – *(hier)* dünn;
to pad – trotten

as the previous one, but this apartment had a balcony. Her Sunday lunch – a **charred** yellow pepper stuffed with mince and tomatoes – was on the table by the window. And beside her plate was a **pair of binoculars**!

"Oh!" cried Isy, pretending to be **dismayed**. "You've already got a pair of binoculars!"

"Was that the prize?" asked Mrs Grigoleit, disappointed.

"I'm afraid so. We'll have to give it to someone else. But your old binoculars look pretty good to me."

"They're made by Zeiss," said the woman proudly. "They belonged to my husband who **passed away**."

"What powerful lenses!" said Isy. "I bet you can see straight into Professor Pioschleck's stylish kitchen ..." She turned to Amanda. "It's a good job Mrs Grigoleit isn't eating scrambled eggs!"

— 26 —

Isy's roast dinner was cold by the time she got home. Worse still, her mother's expression was frosty.

Feeling guilty, she wolfed down her meal.

"Will you be here at teatime or are you aban-

---

charred – verkohlt;
a pair of binoculars – ein Fernglas;
dismayed – verzagt; to pass away – sterben

doning us again?" asked Mrs Schütze. She served Isy some pudding: a bowl of plums in syrup. A delicious smell of cake **wafted** from the kitchen.

"I don't know," muttered Isy, who didn't have the heart to spoil her mother's afternoon. She was supposed to be meeting Tannhäuser and Gummy Bear at the Bornsteins' in an hour. FC Union Berlin were playing **an away game** that Sunday, which meant there was no conflict of loyalties for the boys.

"I baked the cheesecake for you, you know," her mother called from the kitchen. She sounded upset. Isy wished she could tell her the truth. If she were to explain the events of the last few weeks, her mum would understand the importance of the meeting and why she was almost never at home. But Mrs Schütze had to be kept in the dark. She would find out about her daughter's **exploits** from the headlines as usual.

Isy finished her pudding and went to her room. She spent a few moments at her desk, jotting down everything that had happened in an exercise book.

It was the first time she had put anything on paper. At first it hadn't seemed necessary, but things had become so complicated that she was in danger of missing the links. Biting her tongue in concentration, she listed the main points and mapped out the key protagonists, sketching the connections with different felt-tip pens. She start-

---

to waft – wehen;
an away game – ein Auswärtsspiel;
exploit – *(hier)* Abenteuer

ed with Josepha's name in the middle, but crossed it out and swapped it for Lothar Loll. They had found Josepha, so the next step was to collar the criminal.

Loll was bound to have read the morning headlines – in which case he would know that his prisoner had escaped. The question was: how would he react? Would he believe the headlines, or would he suspect that the police were trying to **outwit** him? Would he return to apartment 1101 at the agreed time, or would he disappear without trace? *Whether we catch him,* thought Isy, *depends on what he decides to do now*. She wondered what the boys would make of the situation.

Full of anticipation, she leaned back in her chair and scanned her notes.

She couldn't help feeling triumphant about the fact that she and Amanda knew more about the case than anyone, including Detective Rose. Together they had found Josepha, traced the anonymous phone call, and identified the villain who was pulling the strings.

So much had happened since they **donned** their blonde wings and blue glasses for the first time and began their careers as holiday angels a fortnight ago. She would never have imagined that they would be hot on the heels of the most wanted criminal in Berlin. Without their efforts, not even Josepha would know the truth about Lothar Loll!

---

to outwit s.o. – jmdn. überlisten;
to don – aufsetzen

Isy was determined not to let the end of the holidays **jeopardize** the outcome of the case. She and Amanda would turn up at school on Monday and **take everything in their stride**.

She tore the pages out of her exercise book and stuffed them in her pocket, then crept into the hall and grabbed her parka, ignoring the appetizing smell of warm cake. Her parents were roaring with laughter in the lounge – they were probably watching an old comedy on TV. She closed the door carefully behind her.

It was miserable outside. The grey sky was laden with a chilly dampness that was neither rain nor fog but which fell to the pavement silently, covering the tarmac in a glistening sheen. **Wistfully**, Isy remembered the cheesecake that her mother had made especially for her. To her surprise and delight, she discovered that Amanda had been baking as well. Isy followed her into the Bornsteins' shiny white kitchen where Amanda took up position at the marble worktop and proceeded to sprinkle icing sugar over a Victoria sponge.

"You've got a real talent for this," said Isy admiringly.

"It's not exactly difficult. I made it out of a packet."

"You're still better at it than me," said Isy truthfully. "Shall I get some plates?"

---

to jeopardize – gefährden;
to take s.th. in one's stride – gelassen hinnehmen;
wistful – wehmütig

Amanda looked at her blankly. "What for? I didn't make it for us."

"Oh," said Isy, embarrassed.

"It's for Pio! I'm going to take it to him in jail."

They were interrupted by a sharp ring at the door. Isy was too bewildered to move, so Amanda strode past her and let the boys in.

Tannhäuser and Gummy Bear made the same mistake as Isy. In fact, Gummy Bear, remembering the earlier incident with the scrambled eggs, seemed to think that the cake was Amanda's way of setting things right.

"Hands off!" she said sharply. "It's a present. Besides, it's extremely rich in iron."

"In iron?" drawled Tannhäuser, straightening his baggy T-shirt "Do you mean it's full of **nuts**?"

"I mean it's got a **file** from dad's toolbox inside it," said Amanda proudly. "It looks like an ordinary cake, but Pio will be able to use it for his jailbreak!"

The others fell about laughing.

"Well we've got to do something!" protested Amanda. "We can't just let him **rot** in jail!"

"Haven't you heard? The police let him go. It was on the news just now," said Tannhäuser. "You may as well cut the cake."

Professor Pio had been released! Isy and Amanda hugged each other in relief. It was the best possible present that the boys could have given them.

---

nut – Nuss, (Schrauben-)Mutter;
file – Feile;
to rot – verwesen

Soon there was nothing left of the cake except the hardware. Isy cleared the table and got out her notes. "Lothar Loll is our priority," she explained. "We need to know where he is, what he's thinking, and what he intends to do next."

There was silence while they **pondered** the matter.

"He'll be miles away by now," drawled Tannhäuser after a while.

"If I could get my hands on the interfering **busybody** who told the police about Josepha, I'd decorate his face – and not just with scrambled eggs!" threatened Gummy Bear.

Lara Croft blushed crimson at the mention of eggs.

"It was Mrs Grigoleit," said Isy.

Gummy Bear's eyes practically popped out of his head. "A woman?"

They nodded.

"Do the police know her name?"

"I doubt it," said Amanda, with a nod towards Isy. "Our very own detective tracked her down."

"How did Mrs Grigoleit spot Josepha?"

"She was looking at Pio's apartment through her binoculars. I expect she was just curious about her famous neighbour, but then she saw Josepha – the girl that all Berlin was desperate to find." Suddenly Isy felt sorry for the old woman. "I'm sure she didn't want to land Pio in prison, but what else

---

to ponder – grübeln;
busybody – Wichtigtuer

could she do? For all she knew, Josepha might have been in danger."

"I hadn't thought of it like that," admitted Amanda. "She was trying to **do a good turn**."

"And thanks to her, the real criminal got away," said Tannhäuser.

"What if he hasn't heard the news?" Gummy Bear pushed back his chair and searched the kitchen for an ashtray.

"He told Josepha that he was flying to Bosnia and would be back by Halloween, but he might have been lying," said Amanda.

"I reckon he was here all the time," chimed in Isy. "We'll have to assume that he's heard the news. Still, he might think that the story about Josepha's friendship bracelet is a **ruse**. Everyone knows that the police sometimes plant false stories in the media as a tactic to draw out suspects. The fact that the police are still looking for Josepha might convince him that it was all a lie." She drummed her pen against the table. "I think he'll go back to the apartment. A quarter of million euros are **at stake**! He'll want to see for himself what's going on."

"Hmm," said Tannhäuser **noncommittally**. "Is there a Yellow Pages round here?"

"Sure," said Amanda, leaping up to fetch the heavy book.

---

to do a good turn – einen Gefallen tun;
ruse – Finte, Trick;
to be at stake – auf dem Spiel stehen;
noncommittally – ohne sich festlegen zu wollen

"Brilliant!" exclaimed Isy, who had guessed what Tannhäuser intended to do. If Lothar Loll was a house-clearance specialist, they could track him down through his job. That way they would be able to **apprehend** him regardless of whether he went back to the apartment.

Gummy Bear decided to use the lid of a jam jar as an improvised ashtray. "I don't know why you're bothering to look for him. Why don't we hand Josepha back to her parents and pocket our cash?"

No one answered. Tannhäuser was busy leafing through the Yellow Pages and reading out telephone numbers for Amanda to write down. The list comprised three Berlin companies so far. Meanwhile, Isy was wondering how a bunch of seventh-graders without house or furniture could convince a house-clearance agency to do business with them. Thirteen-year-olds probably weren't their target market.

We need a grown-up to help us, she decided. But whom could they ask without explaining everything from start to finish? *No one,* she thought **dismally**. *Unless …*

She leapt to her feet and hurried out of the kitchen. Her idea was as unripe as a sour apple, but she was determined to give it a shot. Her friend's mobile was lying on her bed under the timid gaze of Prince William who watched over the sleeping Amanda every night. Isy scrolled through the con-

---

to apprehend – festnehmen;
dismal – traurig, düster

tacts, took a deep breath and waited for the familiar voice to answer.

"Hi there! Are you having a good Sunday afternoon? I'm calling on behalf of the calamity queens. Do you mind if we ask you a favour?"

– 27 –

"**What have** I let myself in for?" sighed Mr Rimpau, who had been hoping to spend the sunlit Monday afternoon finishing the final chapter of his latest novel. He could have been working on his manuscript in the peace of his study, sipping a powerful brew of perfumed Darjeeling and **shuffling** combinations of situations, characters and words, but instead he was sharing his lounge with two excitable teenage girls, who had arrived at his apartment straight after school. They were straining to hear the doorbell. In a few moments a complete stranger would arrive and offer to **divest** him off his worldly possessions. He couldn't think why he had agreed to it all.

Following Isy's phone call, he had contacted three house-clearance companies and requested a quote. Thankfully, the girls weren't expecting him to sell his possessions, but the point of the exercise was still unclear. Isy and Amanda were obviously scared of something – the incident with the chest

---

to shuffle – mischen (Spielkarten);
to divest s.o. of s.th. – jmdm. etwas wegnehmen

of drawers had been proof enough of that – but they refused to open up. In fact, they were determined to say as little as possible about today's proceedings. His role was simply to show the clearance agents around his apartment and stick to the questions prepared for him by the girls. With great reluctance they had finally admitted that the two boys hiding in the bushes on the other side of the road were two of their classmates who were waiting for Amanda to **twitch** the woven curtains, at which point they would set off in hot pursuit of the caller.

Mr Rimpau studied Isy and Amanda's pale, tense faces. They were sitting nervously on his antique Biedermeier sofa, tickling Alfredo's furry grey ears.

"Would you like a cinnamon tea?" he enquired, taking pity on them.

At that moment there was a ring at the door, and the girls leapt off the sofa and **scuttled** into the hallway to hide in an alcove draped with burgundy felt. Alfredo barked furiously while Mr Rimpau opened the door to clearance specialist number one.

Meanwhile, Isy and Amanda held hands behind the curtain and listened expectantly to the stranger's voice. It definitely wasn't Wolfram B. Braun.

Long moments passed as Mr Rimpau took the man on a tour of his spacious apartment. The girls

---

to twitch – zucken, zupfen;
to scuttle – huschen

heard snatches of their muttered conversation. The man was obviously excited by the money to be made from Mr Rimpau's priceless antiques, but he was less enthused by the sight of his books. He studied the bookshelves in the study and the hall, and came to a halt in front of the curtain. Isy peered underneath and saw a pair of brown loafers with thick cream soles. "Blimey **governor**, how many books have you got here? I'd have to sell them by the kilo."

"Four thousand or so, I should think," replied Patrick Mortimer Rimpau politely. "But don't worry: I'm taking them with me. So you'll send me your quote?"

"We'll fax it over."

By the sound of the footsteps, Mr Rimpau was escorting the man to the door. "There's one more thing," he said, dutifully sticking to his script. To Isy's satisfaction and relief, he made the questions sound natural.

A moment later Mr Rimpau drew back the curtain. "Nothing out of the ordinary, except the cost of the **call-out**," he reported as they made their way back to the lounge and waited for the next caller. The first man had told Mr Rimpau that none of his colleagues answered to the name of Wolfram B. Braun or Lothar Loll.

"What if your chap turns up at the door?" asked the writer, filling his pipe. "He's not dangerous, is he? What if he finds out you're here?"

---

governor – *(als Anrede)* Chef, Meister;
call-out – Fahrtkosten

He needn't have worried. The next guy was a woman in black **suede** boots with high heels.

Isy and Amanda were taken aback. They hadn't expected the clearance specialist to be a woman, but there was no reason why she couldn't do the job.

Mr Rimpau took the woman on the second tour of his realm. When asked why he was leaving such a beautiful apartment, he replied that he was planning to spend the next few years in the States. "Lucky you," she said enviously. They swapped business cards, then the woman promised to send a quote, and Mr Rimpau posed the scripted questions.

"At our Berlin office?" the woman echoed. "Lothar Loll or Wolfram B. Braun?"

In Isy's imagination, she was raising her eyebrows **quizzically**.

"No, I'm afraid I don't know anyone by either of those names."

They were out of luck again.

The trio regrouped in the lounge. Isy peered out of the window to check on Tannhäuser and Gummy Bear who were trying to keep a low profile behind a row of conifers. She wondered what they had made of the black-booted woman in the white **estate car**. House-clearance specialist number three was due to arrive in an hour, and then they could all go home. The boys looked frozen and were pacing up and down.

---

suede – Wildleder;
quizzical – fragend;
estate car – Kombi

"Why don't we play a game to pass the time?" she proposed.

"Japanese chopsticks, anyone?" asked Mr Rimpau, who enjoyed a good game of Mikado.

The girls giggled.

"Rummy!" suggested Amanda, trying to get in first before Isy bullied them into playing Cluedo.

"Cluedo!" said Isy firmly.

"A fine game of logic," said Mr Rimpau approvingly. "Personally, I'd like to play poker, but I'm afraid we'll have to pass." He shrugged his shoulders apologetically. "My children have raided the games cupboard. It's bad enough when they move out, but then they take everything with them..."

"Don't worry," said Isy. "We can always read instead. It's like a library in here." She paced the bookshelves, scanning the titles attentively. A moment later, she squealed in surprise. "I didn't know you wrote love poetry as well!"

"It's ancient history. But it worked on my wife."

"Can you read us a love poem?" asked Amanda.

"Heaven forbid!" he protested in alarm.

His prayer was answered. At that very moment their visitor rang the doorbell thirty minutes earlier than agreed. The startled girls darted behind the curtain and waited with pounding hearts as Mr Rimpau opened the door to the third caller.

It was their last chance. This time it had to be him!

At first they couldn't hear anything because of Alfredo. Mr Rimpau shut the barking dog in a separate room, and at last they could hear the visitor's voice. To their disappointment, it wasn't their man. Maybe Tannhäuser had got it wrong. What if Wolfram B. Braun, aka Lothar Loll, wasn't a house-clearance specialist?

Isy considered what to do next. Meanwhile, Mr Rimpau set off on the third guided tour of his **hallowed** apartment. He showed the man his antique furniture, shiny new gadgets and priceless china, then asked the usual questions. They couldn't hear the man's replies.

"I see. So you've never heard of Braun or Loll," repeated the author loudly for their benefit. Then the door shut behind the third and final caller.

"That's that, then," sighed Mr Rimpau. "No joy, I'm afraid."

At that moment Isy shot out from behind the curtain like a catapult and rushed past the bewildered author. She caught up with an overweight man of medium height in a navy blue coat who was **negotiating his way** carefully down the stairs.

"Sorry to bother you, but I'm afraid my fri… I mean, my father, asked the wrong question. I know you've never heard of a Wolfram B. Braun or a Lothar Loll, but maybe you've got a colleague who's about the same height as you but slimmer and with brown eyes and dark hair?"

"Dark hair?" The man was still **wheezing** for breath. "All my colleagues are blonde."

---

hallowed – heilig;
to negotiate one's way – sich umständlich einen Weg bahnen;
to wheeze – keuchen

Isy had a flashback to Wolfram B. Braun sitting at his desk and rummaging in his wallet. She remembered how his brown hair had shimmered in the lamplight. It had a definite reddish hue.

"He might have dyed it," she said, trying to keep it short because the man was in a hurry. "He's really into movies. He likes Maximilian Schell."

"Oh, you mean Rainer!" The man in the blue coat chuckled. "Rainer Wutzke. I haven't seen him in months. He's a real movie **buff**. The lads used to call him 'the director'."

"Do you know where he lives?"

"You could ask at the office," he said, taking his leave with an absent-minded nod. He shuffled down the stairs, wheezing softly. Overcome with relief, Isy sat down on the steps. Bingo!

— 28 —

Isy knew that it was going to be a tough day even before she got up.

Lessons would start with Maths, followed by German, Music, and Biology. After that, Amanda would mysteriously develop toothache, twist her ankle or fall into a faint; the choice was hers. In any event, Isy would volunteer to escort her home – and the two of them would hurry over to Otti and Lotti's before making their way to see Gottfried in Karlshorst. They would have to be quick because

buff – Experte

they were scheduled to meet Hagen and Reginald at three o'clock outside apartment 1101. If everything went to plan, they would proceed to overpower Rainer Wutzke, aka Lothar Loll, aka Wolfram B. Braun and hand him over to the authorities.

Later, Mrs von Leinungen would leave Brinkenbühl with 'Harissa' and the four heroes would return the missing girl to her parents.

It was going to be an extremely busy day – and to add to the excitement, it was Halloween!

Isy was exhausted already. Her sleep had been interrupted by another terrifying nightmare.

In her dream, she and Amanda were relaxing in the luxurious library of the Cluedo mansion. Reverend Green burst into the room.

"I assume you've seen Mrs White's corpse in the kitchen?" he said darkly. "We know the place of the murder, but not the weapon. Silver candlestick, **lead** piping, rope, pistol or dagger? Take your pick!"

"But Mrs White isn't the real Mrs White," said Isy, horrified. "Mrs von Leinungen was playing her character!" She ran down the corridor, followed by Amanda and Reverend Green, and stormed into the kitchen. A life-size doll in a white lace apron and grey hair was lying on the chequered tiles. Her old-fashioned **bodice** had been slashed open and was leaking **sawdust** onto the floor.

---

lead – Blei;
bodice – Mieder; sawdust – Sägemehl

It's only a doll, thought Isy. Her relief turned to horror when she realized that Reverend Green was morphing before their eyes. His **sparse** grey hair was already darker and bushier; his flabby body seemed somehow more muscular; and his prominent brown eyes acquired a **ruthless** glint. Rooted with fear, she realized who they were dealing with.

"Mandi, we've been trapped!" she shouted in alarm. "He tricked us! He's not Reverend Green; he's Rainer Wutzke!"

She woke up in a cold sweat and was still shaking while she cleaned her teeth. It was a good job that the case would be closed by this evening.

"Wish me luck, mum," she said, kissing her mother goodbye. She stuffed a length of string into rucksack – they would use it to tie the villain's hands. "If things go well, I won't have to rush around after today. I might even have time to tidy my room!"

"Luck with what? Are you sitting an exam?"

Isy shook her head.

"Then why..."

"Don't worry, mum! I'll be fine!"

I'll be fine, she repeated to herself as she hurried to the trees in front of the supermarket to meet Amanda. There was a smell of snow in the air, and the maples had lost the last of their leaves. A man in blue overalls was sweeping them up. He collected them into a pile in front of the little travel

---

sparse – schütter;
ruthless – unbarmherzig

agent's. Baskets of chestnuts and rosy apples had been placed on display. The shop was advertising holidays in South Tyrol.

"I'd rather fly to the Maldives," said a cheery voice beside her. Amanda's face appeared in the glass next to hers. She shivered and rubbed her hands together. "It's lovely and warm in the Maldives. And we'll be able to afford it as well. I bet Mrs Boskov will add a bit extra to the reward."

"Don't count your chickens before they hatch."

"What chickens?"

"It's a proverb, Amanda! The point is, we haven't caught the **villain** yet."

"Now you come to mention it…" Amanda cleared her throat in embarrassment. "I'm afraid I can't make the meeting this afternoon."

It had started to snow. Isy stared at the falling snowflakes in horror. "You're not serious, are you?"

Amanda hung her head and nodded.

Isy pursed her lips together and didn't say another word, but inside she was furious. What kind of a friend was Amanda? Isy could scarcely believe that she was leaving her in the lurch. *What a **fickle**, unreliable …*

Had Amanda forgotten the long hours spent cleaning carpets, feeding animals, watering plants and stroking cats? Isy had sacrificed her holidays without a word of complaint in order to save Amanda from going to prison for forging a cheque.

---

villain – Bösewicht;
fickle – wankelmütig

She felt sick to the stomach. What could possibly be so important that Bumblebee couldn't deal with it another time? Was she on a date with her mysterious debtor?

Wet clumps of snow pelted Isy's face, stuck to her eyelashes and cooled her burning forehead. Amanda's fringe and eyebrows were dusted with snowflakes, too. Dr Trisch would be surprised to see a pair of walking snowmen in his classroom, but at least Isy and Amanda wouldn't be alone. Two familiar figures had just left the warmth of the bakery next to the **shuttered** windows of the slumbering Georgio's. They were carrying a big bag of treats. In spite of the swirling snowflakes, Isy recognized them as Saskia and Binette.

The four girls walked the rest of the way together. Saskia told the others about a **torrid** love film that she had watched on telly the previous night. Isy was happy to let her talk. In her opinion, anything was preferable to conversing with her **traitorous** best friend, who was walking beside her in silence. Every now and then Amanda stopped and looked back through the falling snow.

"Someone's following me," she whispered. "I noticed as soon as I left home."

Isy was still furious with Amanda, but she couldn't help laughing. "Your guilty conscience is probably stalking you!"

---

shuttered – mit geschlossenen Fensterläden;
torrid – glühend;
traitorous – verräterisch

Amanda waited until they had dusted the snow from their coats and were inside the classroom. "He was wearing a brown hat," she hissed stubbornly. "And anyway, what's the plan? Do you want me to develop toothache, twist my ankle or fall into a faint?"

"It's your choice. But don't do anything until after Biology!"

Predictably, Amanda fell into a faint during the third period, exactly two hours too soon. They were in the middle of a folk song about a **rosebud** when the detective burst into the classroom, as if summoned by the lyrics. Helped by Trischi, he pinned a poster to the board. It featured two female personages with curly blonde hair and matching blue glasses. They were both wearing shapeless capes. The sketch had been drawn by police artists from information provided by Professor Pioschleck's housekeeper and the porter.

Isy could feel the colour draining from her cheeks as she stared at the poster.

Amanda had gone pale, and beads of sweat were forming on Gummy Bear's forehead.

Detective Rose warned the class that two female suspects were operating in Berlin as holiday angels and were urgently wanted in connection with the disappearance of Josepha Boskov. His voice seemed to be coming from very far away.

"They could be students," he was saying, "but

---

rosebud – Rosenknospe

they're probably schoolgirls, as indicated by the fact that they were mainly active during the holidays. We're focusing our enquiries on Josepha's school. I'll be visiting each classroom and displaying the poster. Can anyone identify the suspects?"

"Did anyone see them during the holidays?" **probed** Dr Trisch. "If so, we'd like to know when and where!"

Naturally, no one said a word. Isy stared mutely at her desk. *I should have known this would happen,* she thought glumly. She tried to look inconspicuous.

Dr Trisch brightened up. He had spotted a hand.

"Yes, Jennifer?"

"I saw them!"

Everyone whirled round in their seats to look at Jennifer Niemann, who was looking embarrassed and self-important. "It was last Saturday. I'd just seen a cool yellow top in a boutique, when I noticed them coming towards me. I didn't realize they were supposed to be holiday angels – I thought they were Christmas fairies or something. Anyway, we were almost level, when one them muttered something under her breath."

Jennifer paused, deciding whether to tell the full story. Eventually she decided that she couldn't withhold important information from the police. She would have to tell the truth. "She said something like: 'You can't hide the truth forever'!"

The class exploded into laughter.

---

to probe – bohren

"Did you recognize her voice?" enquired Detective Rose, ignoring the noise.

Jennifer shook her head.

"Did it sound like anyone you know?" the detective asked patiently.

"It sounded... It sounded a bit like Amanda Bornstein," whispered Jennifer, glancing apologetically at her classmate.

If only Amanda had never said anything! Isy's heart skipped a beat. *It's all over now,* she thought desperately. *Amanda will lose her nerve and admit everything.* To her intense relief, her friend paled under Detective Rose's suspicious, prickly gaze, and **toppled** off her chair.

— 29 —

Every year on 31 October the pumpkins came out in force.

Isy had read somewhere that the tradition of dressing up on All Hallows Eve had originated with the Celts, who carved masks from turnips to **ward off** the devil. In the late nineteenth century, thousands of Irish immigrants brought the custom to America. Pumpkins were substituted for turnips, and the smiling symbol of Halloween was born. Over the past few years Berlin had taken to celebrating in the American way as well.

---

to topple – stürzen;
to ward off – abwehren

Windowsills were decorated with pumpkins, trick-or-treaters roamed the streets, and everyone went to **ghoulish** parties. Last year Isy and Amanda had eaten 'Dead Men's Fingers' instead of sausages and danced the 'Skeleton Waltz' and 'Graveyard Polka'.

Mrs Knosalla was familiar with the rituals. No sooner had Isy and Amanda rang her doorbell than she showered them with biscuits, sweets, lollipops and chocolate bars.

"It's only us, Mrs Knosalla," they chorused, **declining** the sweets with good grace. "We're your holiday angels."

Mrs Knosalla did a **double take**. "Why aren't you wearing your beautiful costumes?"

The truth was, Isy and Amanda had disposed of their outfits. After their hasty departure from school, they had rushed home, torn up their wigs, capes and glasses, stuffed the pieces into bags and deposited them in different rubbish bins throughout the city. All evidence of their existence as holiday angels had been destroyed. Needless to say, none of this was destined for Mrs Knosalla's ears.

"I'm afraid we weren't allowed to keep them," said Isy carefully. "How was the spa?"

"I'm a new woman!" declared Mrs Knosalla, raising her freshly plucked eyebrows as she smiled.

---

ghoulish – gruselig;
to decline – ablehnen;
to do a double take – zweimal hinschauen;

Her face was rosy from facials, massages and fresh forest air. "I've never felt so wonderfully relaxed."

She shuffled into the living room where she had started unpacking her winnings. The prizes had piled up in her absence, and they amounted to quite a **haul**: a waffle maker, two bags of **toiletries** containing designer shampoo, a suede briefcase, some matching blue bowls made of glass, a fleecy bathrobe and an oven dish.

"What's the secret of your success?" asked Amanda, impressed. Just then her pink mobile went off and she disappeared into the hallway.

"I was about to ask the same thing," said Isy.

"There's nothing to it really. I can't get a job, you see, and I need to do something with my time. I enter just about every competition I can find." She pointed to a stack of magazines. "I'll start on those later."

She thanked Isy for looking after her goldfish, then produced a wad of notes and threw in the toiletries as a gift. "From Gottfried with love! Goldfish know all about glitter."

"What a kind lady," said Isy to Amanda as they made their way to Otti and Lotti's. The sky looked grey and heavy with snow. "I didn't like her at first, but she was one of our nicest clients."

"I'm going to win some prizes, too," announced Amanda, still **awed** by Mrs Knosalla's success.

---

haul – *(hier)* Fang;
toiletries – Kosmetika;
to be awed – tief beeindruckt sein

"Every magazine contains at least one competition. A week at a beauty spa would be fabulous."

"What do you think Trischi would say to that?" chuckled Isy, glancing at her watch. They were two hours ahead of schedule thanks to Jennifer Niemann, who had **retracted** her momentous accusation after the rest of the class had joined forces to wake Amanda with the help of a **sopping** cloth. Everything was going swimmingly, but Isy still felt uneasy. It hadn't occurred to her until that morning that Rainer Wutzke might be armed. Would Tannhäuser and Gummy Bear be able to overpower him? They had promised to equip themselves with pepper spray, but Isy had her doubts.

Thirty minutes after leaving Mrs Knosalla's apartment, they stopped at a florist's to buy a **posy** for Mrs von Leinungen. To her horror, Isy caught a glimpse of a man in a hat who seemed to be following them. A moment later he was gone. She wondered whether she was still in shock. She hadn't quite recovered from seeing her face on Detective Rose's poster.

I must be imagining things, she thought nervously. Meanwhile, Amanda asked the assistant to make up a small bouquet of tiny purple asters and sweet-smelling **gypsophila paniculata**. She couldn't have made a better choice. Isy was im-

---

to retract – zurückziehen;
sopping – patschnass;
posy – Blumensträußchen;
gypsophila paniculata – Schleierkraut

pressed that her friend had read Mrs von Leinungen's character so well. Amanda was full of surprises.

The first surprise had come a few hours earlier when Amanda had announced a change of plan. On recovering from her fainting fit, she had informed Isy that she would be accompanying her to Lothar Loll's apartment after all.

Isy was too grateful to wonder what had prompted the turnaround, but Amanda was about to surprise her again. As soon as they reached Mrs von Leinungen's door, she handed her a package of cat food in **cling film** and said mysteriously, "I've got to see to something. Can you manage on your own?"

A second later, she was gone. Isy listened in disbelief as the door slammed in the lobby. She remembered that Amanda had answered a call on her mobile. Had Bumblebee rearranged her secret date?

She doesn't want me to know about it, she thought furiously, taking a spoonful of fried chicken, **leek** and bean sprouts from the pan and eating it herself. At least Amanda had prepared Otti and Lotti's meal in advance: whatever her failings, she was never less than **diligent** when it came to the cats. Isy spent the next thirty minutes grooming, changing the litter tray, sweeping the flat and ar-

---

cling film – Frischhaltefolie;
leek – Porree, Lauch;
diligent – fleißig

ranging the flowers on the coffee table next to the sofa. She wanted the apartment to look welcoming when Mrs von Leinungen got home.

She took a last look round while Otti and Lotti followed her progress with their **inscrutable amber** eyes. There was nothing more to be done. The holiday angels would never have to feed another pet or empty another mailbox again. Isy's relief was **tinged** with sadness. Over the past weeks she had grown fond of cheerful old Fred, hard-backed Leila, silent Gottfried, smelly Wolodja, and Mrs von Leinungen's black-and-white gourmet cats.

"Take care of yourselves," she whispered affectionately. "I'll visit soon, I promise." She put on her parka and gave her hair a quick brush. Just then she heard footsteps in the corridor. She had left her key in the door for Amanda to let herself in.

Trust Amanda to turn up when all the work had been done!

"I'm afraid you've missed the fun," she said crossly.

The door opened and Janho von Leinungen stared at her with bright blue eyes. She hadn't reckoned with *him*.

"What are you doing here?" asked Mrs von Leinungen's nephew, frowning. He looked as if he had been hit by a bus. The right side of his face was

---

inscrutable – unergründlich;
amber – Bernstein;
to tinge – schattieren

swollen and scratched, and his forehead was covered with a sticking plaster. His nose looked **battered**, too.

Isy was about to answer back sarcastically when she remembered that Janho wouldn't have recognized the blonde-haired, white-caped holiday angels as Isy and Amanda from 7b.

"Er, I'm one of the holiday angels. But I'm leaving now."

"Nice work," said Janho, grinning all over his wounded face. "What have you done with your frying pan?" He held out a couple of tired-looking pink asters. "They need a vase."

Isy ushered him in. "You look dreadful."

"It was a lot worse three days ago."

Isy took off her parka and hung it on the coat stand. "Don't ask me where your aunt keeps her vases. I'm already using the one on the coffee table."

"It's all right, I know my way around," he said coolly, pushing past her into the lounge. Judging by the slamming and rattling, he was opening every single cupboard and drawer. Isy wondered why he didn't settle for a glass. She went through the kitchen cupboards and examined the glassware. Her gaze fell on a small **jug** with an elegant handle. She studied her reflection in the cupboard door. Her hair was all over the place and she looked a real mess. Meanwhile, the guy whom she couldn't stop

---

to batter – verprügeln, auf jmdn. einschlagen;
jug – Krug

thinking about was in the next room, searching for a vase. Then it occurred to her: maybe he wasn't really looking for a vase!

Isy put down the jug and hurried into the lounge.

By the look of things, she wasn't a moment too soon. Janho had opened Mrs von Leinungen's bureau and was slipping a plastic **sachet** into his jeans.

"Have you found what you were looking for?"

He whirled round guiltily. "What do you mean?"

"You were looking for a vase, weren't you?"

"Yeah, but she must have moved them all." He pointed to a medium-sized cabinet with a stained glass door. "She used to keep them in here."

"What were you putting in your pocket?"

"A handkerchief. God, you're **nosey**!"

"You've got a nerve, Janho von Leinungen!"

"I could say the same about you!"

For a moment there was silence as they sized each other up. Then Isy picked up the flowers and took them to the kitchen. As far as she was concerned, Mrs von Leinungen's nephew could go to hell. He had found his blasted stuff, so he could hurry up and leave! She listened for the sound of the door. Meanwhile, she turned on the tap and left it running until the water was cold. With any luck, the asters would perk up a bit. Maybe Mrs von Lei-

---

sachet – Beutel(chen);
nosey – neugierig

nungen would believe that Janho had brought them as a welcome-home present, but Isy knew that the flowers were just a **ploy**.

"I expect you think that the flowers were just a ploy," said a voice behind her. "Honestly, Isy, you've got me all wrong."

"Oh really?"

"Yes, really! OK, so I came here to fetch something, but I would have brought the flowers anyway. I happen to like my aunt."

"Mrs von Leinungen asked me and Amanda to look after her apartment. You can't come in here and steal things!" said Isy fiercely.

"Steal?!" exclaimed Janho, eyeing her **derisively**. "I wasn't stealing! I was reclaiming my property."

"Thief!" said Isy.

"**Goody two-shoes**!" retorted Janho.

The telephone rang before Isy had a chance to **retaliate**. She almost jumped out of her skin. It was the first time that the telephone had actually rung in any of the apartments that she and Amanda had been looking after.

"It's bound to be your aunt. She's coming home today. Why don't you answer it?"

Janho von Leinungen shook his head vigorously. "No way! She'll have a heart attack! She mustn't know I'm here!"

---

ploy – *(hier)* Vorwand;
derisive – verächtlich; goody two-shoes – Moralapostel;
to retaliate – Vergeltungsmaßnahmen treffen

Isy had no intention of lying **on his behalf**. Mrs von Leinungen had every right to know that her nephew was in the apartment. She hurried purposefully into the lounge and picked up the phone. "Mrs von Leinungen's residence. Isolde Schütze speaking." It was a relief to hear Mrs von Leinungen's cheerful voice on the other end of the line. Apparently, she and Harissa were staying for Reverend Green's Halloween party, and they wouldn't be home until late that night. They were hoping to take part in a fancy-dress procession.

"What are you going as?" asked Isy, intrigued.

"A skeleton!" said Mrs von Leinungen with a chuckle.

"And how about Jos–, I mean, Harissa?"

"She's decided to go as a witch."

It seemed a fitting choice.

"I hope you have a great time," said Isy sincerely. She grinned at Janho who was standing nonchalantly in the doorway. "You'll never guess who's here! One of your nephews popped by with some flowers.... That's right, it's Janho... In any case, he says 'hi'."

"*You'll never guess who's here!*" said Janho as soon as she put down the phone. "Why do girls always **tell on** everyone?"

"I was helping you out, you idiot! Now you've got a chance to put the sachet back!"

"You're a great help, you are! Do you want me

---

on someone's behalf – stellvertretend für jmdn.;
to tell on s.o. – jmdn. verpetzen

to get beaten up again?" Mrs von Leinungen's nephew ran his fingertips over his battered face and looked at her accusingly. "I'm not doing this for fun, you know."

Isy said nothing, so he tried pleading with her. "It's just a couple of pills that I was supposed to be looking after for a friend. My dad found out about them, so I had to get them out of the house. I hid them in Aunt Gudrun's cupboard, but she must have found them and put them somewhere else. My friend wanted them back, but when I asked where they were, Aunt Gudrun went mad." Janho paused and rolled his eyes. "According to her, I'm a junkie and a dealer. She said I was dragging the von Leinungen name through the mud. She even threatened to **flush** the pills down the toilet to save me from moral ruin."

"Wow," said Isy. "Did she really get rid of them?"

"Of course not. I know Aunt Gudrun."

"Your so-called friend isn't afraid to use his fists."

"My friend didn't beat me up! She was in with the wrong crowd and ..."

"You can't let people beat you up! Why don't you go to the police?"

"Because–" Janho bit his lip and fell silent. "I've said too much already." He turned to leave and stopped at the door. "You've got lovely brown eyes, you know."

---

to flush – spülen

Isy blushed bright red. She wasn't sure whether he was **taking the mickey**. "Please, Janho, go to the police. They'll listen if you tell them what's happened."

"I can't. My ex-girlfriend is involved. She made all the arrangements. We were supposed to get 200 euros each for looking after the pills. She's been kidnapped, and they're probably holding her until they get their stupid pills. Now can you understand why it was so important for me to find the stuff?"

"If you're talking about Josepha, there's no need to worry," said Isy calmly. She unhooked her parka from the coat stand and pulled it on. "Your aunt is taking excellent care of her. They're both in the Cluedo mansion in Brinkenbühl, and they'll be back in Berlin tonight."

"Say that again," stammered Janho, confused.

The door swung open, giving Isy and Janho the shock of their lives. Amanda poked her head into the hallway; her cheeks were red from the cold. She looked at Janho, then Isy, and squealed in surprise. "Honestly, Isy, I can't leave you alone for two seconds!"

---

to take the mickey – jmdn. auf den Arm nehmen

– 30 –

The man in the brown hat was still following them.

He **lurked** in doorways, spied on them on the bus, and stuck to them like a shadow; but try as she might, Isy couldn't get a proper look at him. She was willing to bet that it was Rainer Wutzke. He had probably **picked up** Josepha's **scent** and was hoping that her schoolmates would lead him to her hideout. She wondered why he had chosen to wear a hat: it made him more **conspicuous**. It also looked vaguely familiar. She was sure that a character in a movie wore a hat just like it.

She decided against telling her friend that they were definitely being followed: Amanda would only freak out, and one fainting fit was enough for one day.

They weren't far from their meeting place with the boys, when Amanda tugged Isy's sleeve.

"I know it sounds stupid, but I think I saw that guy again."

"He's been following us all day."

"Really? So I wasn't imagining things?" said Amanda, pleased. She beamed contentedly.

"No, I'm afraid not." Isy glanced over her shoulder, but there was no sign of anything unusual, just a crowd of busy people, a young German shepherd dog who was playing with his leash, and three

---

to lurk – lauern;
to pick up a scent – eine Spur finden;
conspicuous – auffällig

small boys dressed in Halloween costumes. But she knew that he was there. "I saw him when we were buying the flowers."

"Do you think it could be…"

"Your precious movie director? More than likely." They continued in silence, weighed down by the news. When they got to the **pedestrian crossing**, Isy had an idea. "Quick, let's shake him off!"

They held hands tightly and darted across the road without waiting for the lights. On reaching the other side, they sprinted into a side street, ran through the open doorway of an apartment block, and found themselves in a deserted courtyard. Panting and wheezing, they scanned their surroundings. It was a dead end. They would have to climb the courtyard's ancient firewall.

"You go first!" ordered Isy. "I'll shove from behind."

"What if there's a guard dog on the other side?"

"There won't be!"

Sighing disbelievingly, Amanda hauled herself over the wall. Isy pushed from below with all her might, then lifted up her arm to throw the leather bag after her. It contained a long, irregular sausage-shaped object wrapped in cardboard. Amanda shrieked in alarm. "Careful, Isy! You can't just throw it like that!"

"Sorry," snapped Isy. From Amanda's reaction, anyone would think there was a bomb inside her

---

pedestrian crossing – Fußgängerübergang

bag, but Isy's **money was on** half a dozen eggs. Her friend had a habit of stocking up on ingredients at the most inconvenient times. She was probably planning to cook one of her trademark dishes. Amanda had discovered her talent for cooking eggs when they were alone in the lodge in Altgrünheide.

"It's all right. I'll carry it on my back." Isy swung the rucksack over her shoulder and took hold of the crumbling brickwork. She pulled herself up and struggled over the wall. They crossed two further courtyards with considerably lower walls, then came to a carwash. They were almost at the apartment.

"Ha, he'll never catch us now!" said Amanda triumphantly.

Isy couldn't share her optimism. If the man in the brown hat was Rainer Wutzke, he would surely have guessed by now that they were **heading for** his apartment. She wondered what he would do next. Would he get there first and lie in wait for them? What if he locked them up and tortured them? She was sure he would do everything in his power to find out where Josepha was hiding. She stopped to consider. Something wasn't quite right. It didn't **add up**.

"It doesn't add up," she said to Amanda as they wiped the sorry remains of the morning's snow on the doormat of the apartment. "The man who was

---

to put money on – wetten auf;
to head for – unterwegs sein nach;
to add up – Sinn machen, stimmen

following us can't have been Rainer Wutzke!" She pushed the damp locks out of her forehead, relieved to have worked out why they were wrong. "We'd forgotten about the angel outfits. Rainer Wutzke doesn't know what we look like. He's only seen us in disguise!"

Amanda thought about it and realized that she was right. "OK, but who was it then?"

"That's the million-dollar question, Amanda."

— 31 —

They arrived at the apartment ahead of schedule. The boys hadn't got there yet.

Weak **strip lights** lit the long corridor. The only sign of life was a kiddie's bike propped outside the apartment where Lia and her mother lived.

If Josepha's information was correct, they had another hour to kill before Rainer Wutzke, aka Lothar Loll, aka Wolfram B. Braun, appeared on the scene. There was no guarantee that he would.

"Shouldn't we wait for the boys?" whispered Amanda.

"We can't **loiter** in the corridor. People will notice!" hissed Isy.

Nervously, she gripped the key that Josepha had given her and inserted it into the lock. The door came open without a sound. It was **eerily** quiet.

---

strip light – Leuchtröhre;
to loiter – herumhängen; eerie – gespensterhaft

"There's nothing like a bit of oil to keep the lock working nicely," said Isy. As soon as the words were out of her mouth they struck her as so **preposterous** that she almost burst out laughing. It was proof that she was really nervous.

"I need the toilet," whispered Amanda. "Can you check the bathroom for me?"

"What do you expect me to find in there? He's hardly likely to be lurking in the bath!" Giggling, Isy stepped into the **stuffy** hall and resisted the temptation to throw open the windows. It would ruin everything if Rainer Wutzke realized that someone was inside.

She peered into the living room; it was empty except for the green sofa and the dusty desk. There was nothing in the kitchen except the bare bones of the cupboards, and the next room had been cleared out as well. Last of all she opened the door to the tiny bathroom and reassured Amanda that Rainer Wutzke wasn't splashing about in the **tub**. "All clear!"

She made sure that the front door was locked, then unpacked the string. She was confident that it was strong enough to serve its purpose.

Amanda disappeared into the toilet and returned a short while later. She placed her leather rucksack gently on the desk and joined Isy on the sofa. They waited in nervous anticipation for Tannhäuser and Gummy Bear's footsteps in the corridor.

---

preposterous – unsinnig;
stuffy – muffig; tub – Wanne

"What are we going to do if he gets here early?"

"I don't know," murmured Isy. "I'm hoping that he won't."

"Do you really think he'll let us tie him up?"

"Not unless Tannhäuser and Gummy Bear spray him with pepper gas."

"If we're lucky, the police will be here in minutes."

"Only if we call them."

Amanda decided to change the subject. "What was Janho doing in Mrs von Leinungen's apartment? Was he telling the truth about the flowers?"

Isy nodded in what she hoped was a **dispassionate** manner.

"That's funny. You both looked so … **agitated**."

"Agitated?"

Amanda frowned suspiciously. "I hope you're not keeping secrets from me, Isolde Schütze."

"What makes you say that? We tell each other everything, don't we?"

They eyeballed each other intently. Isy was determined to stare Amanda out, but voices sounded from the corridor and they both jumped up to usher their classmates inside.

The boys had brought a bright red canister of pepper gas and the welcome smell of fresh autumn air.

"It's designed for use on guard dogs," drawled Tannhäuser. "A single whiff would make a pit bull cry."

---

dispassionate – leidenschaftslos;
agitated – aufgeregt

"You're in safe hands now," said Gummy Bear heroically.

The boys undertook a **solemn** investigation of the **premises**, and Gummy Bear, who clearly fancied himself as a military leader, ordered the others to take up their positions. According to his plan of attack, he was to lurk behind the living room door with the pepper spray, backed up by Reginald in the kitchen and Isy behind the sofa. Amanda was to wait in the **nursery**.

"But I want to be with Isy!" she whined.

"Fine. In that case, Reginald will take the sofa and you two can wait in the kitchen," ruled Gummy Bear.

Disappointed, Isy handed over the string. She wanted to be at the heart of the action, but she knew better than to argue over who did what. In any case, it made sense for her to keep an eye on Amanda and stop her from panicking. Before she took up position in the kitchen, she told the boys about the man in the hat.

"And you're certain it wasn't Wutzke?"

"Wutzke doesn't know what we look like or where we live. The man in the hat followed Amanda to school."

"Who else could it be?"

"No idea."

"It was probably a dirty old man with a taste for

---

solemn – feierlich;
premises – Immobilie;
nursery – Kinderzimmer

chubby girls," said Gummy Bear, glancing at Amanda. "Your trousers are too tight, Roly Poly."

"You can talk, you pig!" Amanda gave him an angry **prod**.

"He'll be here in fifteen minutes," said Tannhäuser, checking his watch. "What's the plan once we've tied him up?"

"Call Detective Prickles. He'll think it's Christmas and Easter all at once!" said Isy, grinning as she pictured the look on Detective Rose's face. "We'll take him with us to meet Josepha and Mrs von Leinungen."

"And then we'll collect the reward," said Amanda, as if anyone could have forgotten about the cash. "We should sell our story to the newspapers. We've given them enough mileage for free."

"Everyone get to their position!" ordered Gummy Bear.

"Shut up and stop being so **bossy**!" hissed Amanda. She and Isy had just reached the kitchen when the doorbell buzzed noisily. Everyone froze. Gummy Bear and Tannhäuser peered nervously at the door. No one had considered the possibility that Rainer Wutzke might not have a key. The ring at the door was completely unexpected.

What do we do now? thought Isy, heart **pounding**. She and the others crept noiselessly into the

---

chubby – mollig;
prod – Stups;
bossy – herrisch;
to pound – stark klopfen

hallway. To her horror, she was incapable of formulating a single useful thought. After a while they heard whispering and giggling. She **expelled** her breath slowly. What a relief!

"They're trick-or-treaters," she whispered. "Does anyone have any sweets?"

"Trick or treat?" chorused two little girls excitedly when Isy opened the door. She handed them some gummy bears, half a packet of biscuits and a few wads of Tannhäuser's chewing gum.

"It's all we've got, I'm afraid."

"That's OK." The kids put the goodies into their bags. They were wearing grey paper cloaks shaped like **bat** wings.

"You're much nicer than the other man."

"What man?"

"The other man. He said: *Push off or I'll give you the scariest fright of your life!*"

"What a mean thing to say," said Isy.

The little girls nodded.

Isy could feel Amanda tugging at her sweater. She took a step forward and tried another question. "Where did you see this man?"

"Here!"

"What do you mean, *here*?"

"In your apartment!"

Isy looked at them sceptically. "The apartments all look the same. Are you sure?"

The elder of the two girls looked at her **pitying-**

---

to expel – *(hier)* auslassen;
bat – Fledermaus; pitying – mitleidig

ly and pointed to the doormat. "Of course we're sure! He had a green doormat!"

Isy was impressed. What a smart kid! She decided to make quite sure. "So you rang the doorbell earlier, did you?"

The girls shook their heads vigorously. "We saw the man going in." They glanced at each other, alarmed. "He wasn't a burglar, was he?"

"Of course not," Isy assured them. "He was probably just the **caretaker**. He can be horribly **grumpy** at times. Have fun!" She closed the door and turned round, disappointed. The other three looked at her expectantly. "Did you hear that? We missed him," she explained.

"You don't really believe them, do you?" frowned Tannhäuser.

"They were little **pip-squeaks**," said Gummy Bear dismissively. "Kids that age talk all kinds of nonsense. My sister is in the third grade, and she's just as bad. According to her, our apartment is inhabited by a **unicorn** who reads Harry Potter in the bath. I've threatened her with a dead arm, but she still says it's true."

Amanda seemed to doubt the story, too. "Why would they ring if the man was so mean to them?"

"They were telling the truth," insisted Isy.

"Prove it!" drawled Tannhäuser.

---

caretaker – Hausmeister;
grumpy – missmutig;
pip-squeak – Winzling;
unicorn – Einhorn

"Exactly," echoed Amanda. "Prove it!"

"All right, I will!" said Isy suddenly. She rushed into the living room, shoved the chair away from the desk, and disappeared under the solid oak table. She emerged a moment later, **squawking** with excitement. "He was here all right. And he's taken your pumpkin, Amanda!"

– 32 –

What on earth did Rainer Wutzke want with a pumpkin?

Of course, that wasn't the **crucial** question. Events had taken an unexpected turn.

Gummy Bear and Tannhäuser couldn't have looked more aggrieved if all their Christmas presents had been confiscated. Their moment of heroism had been ruined.

No one was ready to ask the all-important question: what next?

The oppressive silence was broken by the rustling of cellophane as Gummy Bear tore open a packet of cigarettes. Isy felt like bursting into tears. To think they had come so close!

She pulled herself together. At least they could be proud of themselves for finding Josepha. The Boskovs would be eternally grateful.

---

to squawk – krächzen;
crucial – entscheidend, äußerst wichtig

"God moves in mysterious ways," said Gummy Bear philosophically.

"True, or he wouldn't have created you," snapped Amanda.

"Shut up, you fat **grouse**."

Before Amanda could think of a suitable reply, they were startled by the roar of an electric drill. It sounded as if someone was drilling through the wall. Tannhäuser got up from the sofa. "We may as well get out of here."

"We've done all we can," agreed Gummy Bear. "Let's collect our reward."

"You haven't earned your share yet!" protested Amanda, glancing at her friend for support.

"We'll do the maths later when we've got the reward," ruled Isy. "Josepha won't be back from Brinkenbühl until this evening. She and Mrs von Leinungen are at a Halloween party at the mill."

"I vote we go home and wait," said Gummy Bear.

"What about the man in the hat? He knows where I live!" objected Amanda.

"Find somewhere else to go," said Gummy Bear unsympathetically.

"**Thanks a bunch**."

"He probably wasn't even following you," said Tannhäuser while Isy locked the door behind them.

"Oh yes he was!" insisted Isy and Amanda in unison.

---

grouse – Schneehuhn;
thanks a bunch! – *(ironisch)* tausend Dank!

"He was following us all right," said Isy. "I saw him as well. He shadowed us for hours."

"And it definitely wasn't Rainer Wutzke?"

"I told you earlier," said Isy impatiently, pressing the button for the elevator. "He's only seen us in our angel outfits. He can't possibly know where we live."

"What if he followed you home one morning when you dropped off the shopping?"

"How could he?" said Amanda sceptically. "We went to half a dozen apartments after that."

"And anyway," added Isy, "why would he suspect us? He only hired us because he thought we were too stupid to notice what was going on. The furore about the friendship bracelet would have come as quite a shock. From then on, he would have been forced to keep an eye on the apartment. He probably thought the police were lying, but he still would have checked."

She broke off for a moment while an old lady stepped out of the elevator, followed by a miniature dog in a purple raincoat. The four classmates piled in.

"He must have noticed that, in **violation** of their agreement, the holiday angels weren't delivering to the apartment anymore. That was his next problem. What if Josepha was still in there and starving to death? He had to keep the appointment in order to find out. But the little bird with the golden feathers had flown …"

---

violation – Verletzung

"He probably thinks she got bored and ran away," said Gummy Bear.

"Hardly! It wouldn't explain the big fat pumpkin!"

"Pumpkin number three," clarified Amanda in a **mournful** voice.

Tannhäuser turned to the girls. "Josepha's only contact with the outside world was you. If you'd helped her to escape, she might have told you about the appointment. I reckon he was waiting for you to show up. He was probably monitoring the elevator to see whether you got out on the eleventh storey, as expected."

"You know what that means, don't you?" said Gummy Bear.

"What?" enquired Amanda innocently as the elevator continued its descent.

No one answered. Isy and the boys exchanged looks.

The elevator stopped twice before it reached the ground floor. Tannhäuser got out and waited by the metal colony of mailboxes in the vestibule. A crowd of noisy teenagers in Halloween masks was **milling about** on the street.

"It changes everything. He could even be watching us now."

"I've been telling you that since this morning," complained Amanda.

A man in a navy cap pushed open the front door,

---

mournful – klagend;
to mill about – zwecklos umherirren

followed by two small boys who were swinging their lanterns proudly. A cold gust swept the glass-walled vestibule.

"Listen, Roly Poly, we're not talking about your brown-hatted stalker," explained Gummy Bear. "Reginald was referring to the other guy."

"But..." began Amanda, then stopped. Which other guy? Was Rainer Wutzke trailing them as well?

"Why don't we **reel** him **in**?" said Isy, her confidence flooding back.

She closed her hand around the string in her jacket pocket. They weren't beaten yet!

"You could probably get him to follow you anywhere," **mused** Tannhäuser. He stepped back to let a red-haired woman empty her mailbox. She **teetered** away in green patent boots.

"Remind me what he looks like."

Isy and Amanda furnished him with a full description of Rainer Wutzke, aka Lothar Loll, aka Wolfram B. Braun. "He might have dyed his hair, though," added Isy.

"The question is, where do we go? We could take him to Potsdam Square, do a **lap** of the Sony Centre, then find a dark corner of the Tiergarten and **wrestle** him to the ground."

"Too many policemen," said Gummy Bear dis-

---

to reel s.o. in – an Land ziehen;

to muse – sinnieren;

to teeter – schwanken;

lap – Runde;

to wrestle – ringen

missively. "I'm in favour of the zoo. We spent enough time there last spring."

"I vote we lock him in the lion enclosure until Detective Rose arrives!" said Isy, laughing. "I'm afraid the zoo closes early in winter. It's only open for another half an hour. The apartment was our safest bet …"

"Why don't we take him to Roly Poly's luxury **condominium**?" suggested Gummy Bear. "Your parents are out, aren't they, Mandi?"

"Are you out of your mind?" hissed Amanda, who had finally grasped what was going on.

"Have you got a better idea? We need to get hold of him somehow!"

Isy knew that Gummy Bear was right. She stared thoughtfully at the **dusky** street. The noisy pumpkinheads had moved on to the next apartment block. She wondered whether Rainer Wutzke was spying on them already. Did he know what she looked like without her blonde wig?

Isy was feeling slightly **queasy**. *What if I'm imagining things?* She decided that the odds of Wutzke following them were no greater than fifty-fifty. But fifty-fifty was fifty per cent, and that was enough to **galvanize** her into action.

"He's the most wanted man in Berlin," said Gummy Bear, yawning. "If I were him, I'd be in-

---

condominium – Appartement;
dusky – dämmernd, dunkel;
queasy – unwohl, übel;
to galvanize – *(hier)* anspornen

credibly careful. He's too smart to let us reel him in. Not unless we take him to Josepha."

"A fat lot of good that would do," muttered Tannhäuser.

"That's it!" said Isy. The others stared at her. There was an unmistakable note of triumph in her voice. They waited to hear her latest brainwave. "We'll reel him in on a very long line! A line that reaches all the way to Brinkenbühl! Rainer Wutzke will be accompanying us to Reverend Green's party!"

– 33 –

Isy hadn't grasped the breathtaking **audacity** of her plan until she saw the others' faces.

"You've got to be **kidding**," stuttered Amanda, shocked.

"It'll never work," grunted Gummy Bear.

"Maybe we can make it work," said Tannhäuser, scratching his head. "We need a car for starters. The bus service is too infrequent, and we can't wait around for hours."

Isy rewarded him with a smile. At least Tannhäuser didn't think she was crazy. "I might be able to work something out," she told them.

She dragged Amanda away from the boys. "Be honest, Amanda. Is Ruky in town with a stolen Fiat?"

---

audacity – Kühnheit; to kid – spaßen

Bumblebee looked like she'd been struck by a **bolt from the blue**. Her face went white, then green, then red. The final colour was a **fetching** blend of strawberries and cream.

"I beg your pardon?" she said hoarsely. "I don't know what you're talking about!" The surprise attack had left her practically speechless.

"We need to get to Brinkenbühl and we can't afford a taxi," said Isy. "I know it's none of my business, but Ruky owes you a favour. I had a feeling he might be in Berlin …"

Long moments passed and neither of them said anything.

"Please, Mandi," begged Isy.

"For your information, Ruky isn't in Berlin, and he certainly won't be picking us up in a Fiat! He doesn't break into cars anymore. In fact, he doesn't drive anymore because he hasn't got a driver's licence, and he can't get a driver's licence because he isn't eighteen. And I'm tired of getting him out of trouble – and so is Doreen. She'll dump him if he messes up again."

Doreen was the baker's fair-haired daughter from Altgrünheide. "Is he still seeing Doreen then?"

"Apparently so," said Amanda sulkily, **stomping** back to join the boys who were passing the time with a cigarette.

---

bolt from the blue – Blitz aus heiterem Himmel;
fetching – *(hier)* attraktiv;
to stomp – stapfen

Isy wondered who else might be able to help them. The most **obliging** of their acquaintances was Patrick Mortimer Rimpau, but the talented writer had a habit of seeing straight through them. He would guess that **something was up** and do everything in his power to keep them out of danger – even if it meant tying them to his Biedermeier sofa. Besides, Isy felt guilty about **distracting** him from his work. Mr Rimpau had suffered enough. She tried to remember if anyone owed her a favour. Only one person came to mind …

"Can I borrow your mobile?" she asked Amanda. Signalling for the boys to follow, she led the way out of the warm apartment block and joined the bustling crowds braving the wind and **slush** of the Alexanderplatz. They walked slowly and unhurriedly, as if they were out for a gentle stroll. They wanted to make sure that Rainer Wutzke would be able to follow them.

If he's following us at all, thought Isy glumly. She had a vision of him sitting at home, watching TV, while they traipsed through the streets for no good reason. She sensed that the others shared her **misgivings**, but they had to do something. They didn't have a Plan B.

They headed for the World Time Clock, a

---

obliging – zuvorkommend;
something is up – es ist etwas los;
to distract – ablenken;
slush – Schneematsch;
misgiving – Befürchtung

favourite romantic hangout even in weather like this. At last the call connected.

To Amanda's irritation, Isy didn't greet the person by name.

"Hi there! You owe me and Amanda a favour, don't you? … Yes, that's right … No, not tomorrow … It won't cost you … We just need you and your car … No more than three hours, I promise …"

Amanda had no idea who was on the other end of the phone or whether the bullying tactics had worked, but she wasn't surprised to see Isy's satisfied expression when she handed back the mobile.

Amanda knew what her friend was like: she could walk all over people when it suited her!

Still, it was baffling how Isy had found out that Ruky was in Berlin. Amanda could only assume that she had followed her to Georgio's and seen Ruky hand over the money.

Dusk had fallen, and the streetlights were **ablaze**. Tiny flakes of snow, no bigger than grains of polenta, descended from the violet evening sky. The tip of Amanda's nose was almost frozen. She thought **longingly** of her parents' nice warm lounge. If only she could be watching a romantic comedy on telly and snacking on crisps! Thanks to Isy, she had to **resign herself to** rushing around in the cold and dark instead. She took a good look behind her. It was just as she had thought: no one was following them, not even the man in the hat!

---

ablaze – hell erleuchtet; longing – sehnsüchtig;
to resign o.s. to s.th. – sich mit etwas zufrieden geben

All the same, she knew her crazy friend would never give in.

As transparent as lemon-flavoured Sprite, thought Isy, who knew exactly what Amanda was thinking. *I bet she's wondering how I knew about Ruky.*

She decided to announce the news. "We're being picked up in ten minutes from the car park outside Kaufhof!"

They wandered up and down for a bit, then it was time to meet their chauffeur. He was waiting for them and wearing his **surliest** expression. He didn't notice them initially because they weren't wearing blonde wigs and blue glasses. Isy waved to him as they approached.

He was acting like they had never met before – which in a sense they hadn't. He got straight to the point. "Where am I taking you?" The wind **ruffled** his dark hair and tugged at the yellow scarf around his neck.

"To a party in Brinkenbühl," said Isy. "Don't worry, we'll make our own way back."

She could barely stop staring at the keys in his hand. It was like a miracle. Ten minutes ago she had dreamed up a strategy for getting hold of a car, and now Max was here in his Hyundai. There was something almost eerie about it, as if she had special powers. Even more scarily, they were about to reel in the most wanted criminal in all Berlin!

---

surly – verdrießlich;
to ruffle – kräuseln

— 34 —

Max seemed like a different person as soon as he was behind the wheel. He steered the blue Hyundai out of the city and was chatty and relaxed.

Admittedly, he wasn't too pleased about being treated like a taxi service by a couple of teenage girls, but his irritation turned to excitement at the thought of the evening ahead. "What sort of party is it?" he asked hopefully. He **twiddled** with the radio and glanced in the mirror. "Is something wrong?"

"I think someone's following us," said Isy cagily. She had no intention of telling Max the full story. It would only make things worse.

"Wow! Do you know who it is?"

"We're working on it," growled a voice from the seat beside him. Hagen Golz was sitting in the front, while Isy, Amanda and Reginald were crammed in the back. Isy had been hoping that Amanda would congratulate her on **getting even with** Max, but Amanda was sulking.

Dark rows of trees, brightly lit windows and deserted fields flashed past. Clouds were flitting across the **pallid** moon.

Isy kept her eyes on a Golf that kept overtaking them and dropping back. A taxi and a white Opel seemed similarly intent on keeping them in their sights.

---

to twiddle – müßig herumdrehen;
to get even with s.o. – mit jmdm. abrechnen; pallid – fahl

"I think he might be driving a Golf."

"Everyone in Berlin drives a Golf," said Gummy Bear **disparagingly**.

"But no one else has overtaken us twice in half an hour," reasoned Isy.

"What about the white Opel?" said Tannhäuser. "And the taxi has been following us, too. There's no reason why he couldn't have **hailed** a cab."

Max was finding the conversation rather childish. "What kind of party is it?" he asked, going back to his original question. "Will there be lots of hot chicks?"

"It's a Halloween party, but they'll all be too old. They're pensioners," replied Isy, thinking on her feet.

"I see," said Max, who was baffled by the explanation. It seemed unlikely that a bunch of teenagers would be going to a party in an old people's home, but he decided to drop Isy and Amanda in their **godforsaken** village and make his escape. After that, he wouldn't owe them any more favours and he could make the most of the evening. He certainly didn't intend to spend Halloween with a load of pensioners.

Max swore under his breath. It was snowing again, and the road was icing over. They continued in silence until a Golf appeared behind them through the cloud of swirling snowflakes.

---

disparaging – geringschätzig;
to hail – durch Handzeichen ein Taxi herbeirufen;
godforsaken – gottverlassen

"It's him again," whispered Isy. "He's right behind us."

"He's wearing a hat," squealed Amanda, **craning** her neck. "I hope you're sorry for laughing at me this morning!"

"He's not wearing a hat!" replied Isy firmly although she couldn't actually be sure. The Golf had dropped back again.

"No one gets past me – with or without a hat!" declared Max. He wondered whether the kids were really being followed, then decided not to get involved. "How much further is it?"

"Thirty minutes at most. The road goes through the woods," said Tannhäuser.

Precisely thirty minutes later the blue Hyundai pulled up outside the brightly lit entrance to the mill. "Wow! What an amazing old people's home! I wouldn't mind spending my **twilight years** in a place like this."

"Why don't you come in and wait?" suggested Amanda.

Max smiled in amusement. "Are we quits?"

"Absolutely," said Isy, shaking his hand. "Thanks for the lift."

They watched as he drove round the turning circle and disappeared into the woods. The rear lights were swallowed by the darkness. Isy realized that she hadn't seen another vehicle since they left the main road: no Golf, no Opel and no taxi. Still, the

---

to crane – recken;
twilight years – Lebensabend

tree-lined country lanes were too dark and windy for her to draw any firm conclusions. Deep in thought, she followed the others to the entrance and pushed open the wooden door.

– 35 –

The mansion was huge – big enough to get lost in – and everything about it was impeccably stylish. It was Tannhäuser and Gummy Bear's first visit to the property, and they looked around with starry eyes. The mansion was **divine**! To think that Josepha, aka Harissa, had been living in the lap of luxury all this time!

There was no sign of anyone in the hallway, but someone was playing the piano in the lounge. They heard **snatches** of laughter, music and conversation from the other rooms. Two elderly ladies wearing pink bat wings scuttled across the marble floor.

"Brilliant idea about the old people's home," said Tannhäuser to Isy. "But what kind of a place is this?"

"Haven't you guessed yet?" replied Amanda smugly. "Isy and I worked it out for ourselves."

At that moment the piano stopped playing, and Reverend Green hurried towards them in a batman costume.

I hope he doesn't recognize us, thought Isy, re-

---

divine – himmlisch;
snatch – Bruchstück

membering how he had spotted them from the upstairs landing. It was a good job that they had been wearing their uniforms at the time.

"Ah, our first visitors," he greeted them warmly. "Come and enjoy the party while we're waiting for the procession to start. Don't forget to help yourselves from the buffet!"

So saying, he threw open the doors to the dining room to reveal a vast wooden table spread with plates of crispy chicken drumsticks, tasty meatballs, mouth-watering salads and a hollow pumpkin containing some spicy-smelling soup. The dagger sparkled on the polished dresser.

"Is it real?" asked Tannhäuser, testing the blade on his thumb. It was deadly sharp.

"This is my kind of party," growled Gummy Bear, **pouncing on** the burgers.

Isy helped herself to a pretzel from the basket and turned to Tannhäuser. "Did you see anyone following us?"

"I'm not sure. Every now and then I thought I saw a car behind us. Sometimes I thought I saw two of them, but then they were gone." Tannhäuser took a nervous taste of the soup. "They must have taken a different turning or carried on without their lights, which isn't exactly safe."

"Can people really drive without headlights?"

"Sure, but they might crash."

"Keep an eye out for anyone who fits our description," she instructed, marching over to the

---

to pounce on s.th. – über etwas herfallen

chicken drumsticks and dragging Amanda away. "Come on, we need to find Josepha and Mrs von Leinungen. The food will taste better when you've worked up an appetite!"

Amanda **reluctantly** followed her friend out of the dining room. They peered into the lounge where a few middle-aged guests dressed in Halloween costumes were sipping **lurid** cocktails and chatting on the pink sofa. None of them looked like Mrs von Leinungen or Josepha. A few ghouls were dancing in the ballroom, but there was no sign of anyone else. A maid offered them a glass of orange juice.

Isy politely declined. "No thanks, but maybe you can help us. We're looking for Mrs von Leinungen."

"She's packing her suitcase. You'll find her in room 12."

They shouted a hurried thank you, charged up the stairs and knocked impatiently on Mrs von Leinungen's door.

It took a few moments for her to open up. She looked puzzled.

"It's only us, Mrs von Leinungen. Isy and Amanda – your holiday angels!"

Mrs von Leinungen took a step backwards, but seemed pleasantly surprised. "Well, well. I wouldn't have recognized you!"

"We're not in uniform today. Is Harissa here?"

---

reluctant – widerwillig;
lurid – grell

"She wanted a swim before the procession."

"Where's the swimming pool?"

"In the basement. There's a fitness centre down there."

They rushed down the stairs to the ground floor where the villagers were starting to arrive. Everyone seemed to be having a fabulous time. There were lots of witches and skeletons, not to mention a few people wearing pumpkinheads with holes cut out for the eyes and mouth. Isy liked the children's costumes best, and at one point she thought she **glimpsed** the friendly bookseller from the village among the milling mass. Reverend Green was standing at the foot of the stairs and **furnishing** the revellers with pumpkin lanterns.

"Do you really think Rainer Wutzke followed us here?" whispered Amanda dubiously. "I know you *want* him to be here, but what are the **odds**?"

"Quite good, according to Reginald. He thinks he saw lights behind us in the woods."

"What about the man in the brown hat?"

"I wish you'd ask me something I knew the answer to!" said Isy, sighing.

They found the entrance to the basement and hurried past the storeroom and the wine cellar until they got to a glass door that led into the fitness centre. It was equipped with a sauna, a solarium, a gym and a pool. A fish was swimming in the

---

to glimpse – einen kurzen Blick erhaschen;
to furnish – ausstatten;
odds – Wahrscheinlichkeit *(bei einer Wette)*

clear blue water. On closer examination, it turned out to be Dr Ursula Schley.

"We're looking for Harissa!" they **bellowed**.

The dentist swallowed a mouthful of water and came up coughing and spluttering. "She left a while ago," she said. She swam a few strokes of freestyle and stopped at the end of the pool. "Isn't it time you came in for a check-up?"

Isy and Amanda were already out of earshot. They searched the sauna and solarium, then returned to the hall. The procession of guests and visitors had gathered outside and was about to leave the mansion to the accompaniment of a skeleton band. The lounge and the ballroom were empty and the only people in sight were wearing pumpkin masks. Isy had just decided to look for the boys when Amanda pointed to a sign above the conservatory. It was the only place in the mansion where guests were permitted to smoke. Without a word, the two friends yanked open the door to the conservatory – but Josepha wasn't there.

Two people, a witch and a pumpkinhead, were standing side by side at the window, watching the procession file past outside. Disappointed, Isy and Amanda stepped back into the corridor. Suddenly, the couple pushed past them and marched towards the front door. It occurred to Isy that the witch bore a striking resemblance to Josepha. Before she had time to draw any conclusions, Amanda was shouting at the top of her voice. "He's wearing my

---

to bellow – brüllen

pumpkin! He stole pumpkin number three with the **knobbly** ear!"

Everything happened at once: the man in the pumpkinhead whirled round, the witch pulled away from him, and Isy squealed "Josepha!" in surprise. By the looks of it, the 'director' had followed them after all.

It was only then that they realized that their schoolmate's wrists were **bound**. A handkerchief prevented her from calling out. Rainer Wutzke must have pounced on her in the conservatory. He knew that Josepha was a smoker. To their horror, the girls realized that they had delivered her into his hands.

Cool-headed Isy who had planned everything so calmly was thrown into a panic. She was learning the difference between theory and practice.

"Somebody help us!" she yelled desperately. She turned to face the criminal. "Let Josepha go!"

"Call the police!" screeched Amanda. "The villain stole my pumpkin!"

Josepha redoubled her efforts to escape from Rainer Wutzke's powerful arms. She aimed a kick at his **shins**. At that moment, a Halloween vampire raced down the stairs, intent on joining the procession. He clearly didn't believe that the girls were in trouble because he waved at them cheerily and carried on.

---

knobbly – knubbelig;
to bind / bound / bound – fesseln;
shin – Schienbein

Isy wondered where Gummy Bear and Tannhäuser had gone. The **brass band** was still playing outside and drowning out their screams. She tried desperately to come up with an idea. She knew that they had to distract the criminal, but how?

"**Turn yourself in**!" she shouted. "You'll never get away with this. We know who you are – and so does Josepha. Your name is Rainer Wutzke and you work for a house-clearance company. We'll tell the police everything we know!"

Afterwards, when everything was over, she said it was the equivalent of **poking** a wasp's nest with a stick.

At the time, she was too busy dealing with the situation to think about analogies. With a furious howl, Rainer Wutzke opened the nearest door and shoved Josepha inside. It happened to be the study next to the library. He locked the door and turned his attention to Isy and Amanda, who ran for their lives.

They sprinted down the seemingly endless corridor, their rucksacks bumping wildly on their backs. At last they reached the kitchen and slammed the door behind them. Rainer Wutzke's heavy footsteps were getting closer. They couldn't lock him out because the door wouldn't bolt, so their only option was to escape via the elegant

---

brass band – Blaskapelle;
to turn oneself in – sich der Polizei stellen;
to poke – *(hier)* stochern

wooden panel beside the sink. Three weeks ago they had stepped out of the secret passage into the kitchen, but now they fled in the opposite direction just as Rainer Wutzke threw open the kitchen door.

– 36 –

It was quiet in the underground passage – quiet, and stuffy. The only sound was the thunderous echo of their footsteps. Isy and Amanda were running **at full tilt**.

They kept running even though they were gasping for air. They kept running even after they got a stitch. Faces **straining** with effort, they raced through the tunnel and glanced nervously back. Had Rainer Wutzke discovered the secret door? Was he chasing them already?

The tunnel was every bit as long as it had been on their first visit. It seemed to go on forever. They raced round a **dimly** lit corner, and something fell out of Amanda's jacket. It was small, brown and round, and looked suspiciously like a meatball.

She stopped to stuff it hastily into her pocket and sprinted to catch up with Isy. In her mind she was running a 600-metre race in PE, only this time she was wearing a rucksack and running for her life.

Lara Croft would have managed the high-speed

---

at full tilt – mit ganzer Kraft;
to strain – anspannen;
dim – undeutlich

chase without breaking into a sweat. Inspired by her heroine's example, Amanda discovered **hitherto** unsuspected reserves of strength. She and Isy only paused for breath when the door to the study came into view. They were almost at the end of the tunnel.

"He's every bit as dangerous as we thought," gasped Isy, who had looked through the almond-shaped slits in the pumpkin and seen the maniacal glint in Rainer Wutzke's eyes. She wondered how long she had been under the sinister **surveillance** of the pumpkinhead.

"What are we going to do?" asked Amanda in a small voice.

"The good news is that we're going to rescue Josepha from the study. The bad news is that we'll have to escape via the kitchen."

"We're trapped," howled Amanda. "I hope you're satisfied now!"

"I wanted to apprehend him!" retorted Isy fiercely. "That's why we came here, Amanda! It wasn't about the reward. We didn't want a dangerous criminal like Rainer Wutzke **on the loose**!"

She was still committed to their mission – but she hadn't reckoned with it being so difficult. Catching a criminal was a lot harder than it seemed. To think that she had planned to **restrain**

---

hitherto – bisher;
surveillance – Überwachung;
on the loose – frei herumlaufend;
to restrain – bändigen

Rainer Wutzke with a bit of string! She wondered whether she should have **confided in** Mr Rimpau after all. There was no telling what Wutzke would do to get his hands on Josepha and the money. Detective Rose should have been tracking him like a bloodhound, but instead he was puzzling over a picture of two girls in blonde wigs and white capes. He would have rescued them if he had known.

Isy wished that she had given the detective more of a helping hand, but it was no good thinking about that now. They would have to deal with Rainer Wutzke on their own.

She listened intently, but there was no sound of any activity in the tunnel. They darted up the steps and pushed against the brickwork with all their strength. The secret door was harder to open than expected, but it shifted enough to allow them to leave the tunnel and step into the comfort of the house. Holding their breath and grinning triumphantly, they entered the study. Their sudden appearance on the oriental carpet took Josepha by surprise. She stared wide-eyed from the purple leather armchair where she was trembling with fear. Only the handkerchief prevented her from screaming at the top of her voice.

"You might want to cancel the appointment for your nose job," said Amanda snidely as they untied Josepha's wrists and took off her **gag**. Josepha didn't say a word. Isy suspected that she was still in shock.

---

to confide in s.o. – sich jmdm. anvertrauen;
gag – Knebel

And Amanda's tactless comment would hardly have helped.

"It's all right, Josepha! You'll soon be safe," she whispered, trying to reassure the startled girl. She kept an eye on the locked door, expecting Rainer Wutzke to come in from the hallway. It was lucky that he wasn't a fan of Cluedo, otherwise he would have known about the tunnel and found them already.

The next step was to formulate a plan of escape. "Is anyone around who could help us?"

Josepha shook her head glumly. "They're all part of the procession."

"How long will they be gone?"

Josepha paused to consider. She was still wearing her silk witch's blouse. "An hour at least."

A whole hour, thought Isy, dismayed. If only there was an adult around to help them! She thought of Dr Schley **ploughing** up and down the pool in her white swim cap. If they could make it to the basement, Josepha would be safe. Wutzke would never dare to lay hands on them in the presence of an adult.

"Are you all right to walk?" she whispered. To her relief, Josepha nodded. "In that case, we'll go back through the tunnel. You can hide in the kitchen and we'll run for help."

"I don't want to go back through the tunnel," whined Amanda. She pointed to the window. "Can't we go that way instead?"

---

to plough – pflügen

"We won't be able to close the window after us, so he'll know how we escaped. If we use the tunnel, he'll think Josepha has vanished into thin air." Isy smiled **wryly**. "He thinks Cluedo is for kids, so he'll never find the secret door. I bet he won't even guess that he's in a Cluedo mansion. It gives us the advantage. Come on, we're running out of time!"

The sound of pounding footsteps in the corridor **underscored** the urgency of her words. Amanda paled and dived into the tunnel uncomplainingly. Isy shoved Josepha after her and closed the secret door behind them.

This time they walked **briskly** instead of running. Hardly daring to breathe, they peered through the wood panelling into the kitchen. As expected, Rainer Wutzke was nowhere to be seen.

"He's probably lurking in the corridor," whispered Isy. "More likely than not, he'll be waiting **in the vicinity** of the dining room. That way he'll be able to see in both directions and keep us away from the boys. He wants to split us up."

"But Tannhäuser and Gummy Bear could easily overpower him!"

"Sure, but he's wearing a pumpkinhead. They won't know it's him!"

"How are we supposed to get out of here if he's monitoring the corridor?"

"We'll have to rely on our **wits**." Isy darted to

---

wry – schief;
to underscore – unterstreichen; brisk – forsch;
in the vicinity – in der Nähe; wits – Verstand

the broom cupboard and inspected it critically. Luckily, it wasn't completely full. "Can you squeeze in there, Josepha?"

"I'd rather stick with you."

"No, it's safer if you stay out of sight," said Isy sternly. "He can't afford to hurt any of us while you're still missing, and he won't find you here!"

"But the bus leaves in half an hour!"

"If we handle this right, you can call your parents and ask them to pick you up."

"We could always take the Rolls," suggested Amanda, rolling the '*r*' luxuriously.

The Halloween witch looked sceptical. "Are you sure this is a good idea?" she asked, fighting for space with the scrubbing brushes and brooms. There wasn't enough room to stand upright, so she crouched at the back of the cupboard. But any amount of discomfort was better than falling into Rainer Wutzke's hands.

"Try not to panic," whispered Isy. "I'm going to lock the door. It won't be for long, I promise." She checked that the cupboard was firmly closed.

"I'd advise you not to smoke in there," hissed Amanda through the keyhole. Meanwhile, Isy was rummaging through her rucksack. Amanda watched in bewilderment as she fished out Mrs Knosalla's bag of toiletries and tore open the plastic packaging with her teeth.

"Leave your mobile here, Mandi," she ordered. "The damn thing will only give us away."

She unscrewed a tube of shimmering apricot shampoo and, holding it upright like a candle, crept to the kitchen door. She signalled for the reluctant Amanda to follow. As predicted, Rainer Wutzke was standing in the corridor. His head was turned in the opposite direction.

Isy realized that the **unwieldy** pumpkin would limit his peripheral vision. She was comforted by the thought.

"On the count of three, we'll make a dash for the lounge," she whispered. "One, two, three!"

They darted out of the kitchen and slipped into the lounge. Isy peered out, eyeing a room on the opposite side of the corridor. Amanda could tell what she was planning: their next stop would be the ballroom, from where they would take another secret passage. It was a move that Isy was particularly fond of making on the Cluedo board. "One, two, three!" she whispered, and they sprinted across the corridor and into the ballroom. Hands trembling, they pushed aside the yellow rattan sofa and found the entrance to the tunnel. It was almost like being part of the board game. Isy was really impressed by the house.

But there was no time to waste. Gasping, they ran down the tunnel towards the conservatory, listening to the thudding of their hearts.

Everything depended on whether they could get from the conservatory to the fitness centre without being seen. There was no direct link between the tunnel and the basement: a secret tunnel that opened out into a cellar wouldn't be secret for long.

---

unwieldy – unhandlich

Worn out from running, they staggered up the steps and pushed **frantically** against the brickwork, hoping to find the secret door that opened into the conservatory. The mechanism was harder to locate than in the study, and Amanda had almost given up hope when a gap opened and they were able to slip through.

Relieved, they **sneaked** into the room. Amanda felt like collapsing on the green armchair. She was ready to drop from exhaustion and only her fear of Rainer Wutzke gave her the strength to carry on.

"Not far now," whispered Isy encouragingly. It seemed ages since their first visit to the mansion when they had climbed through the window in search of Mrs von Leinungen. They had been terrified of what they might find.

Once again, she tiptoed to the door and peered into the hall through a crack in the door. Last time she had heard clinking glasses and tinkling laughter, but now the mansion was ominously still. It took her a while to spot the orange pumpkinhead. Rainer Wutzke was scanning the library. Isy almost giggled at the thought that he was hunting for them among the books. He was welcome to search for as long as he liked. It meant she and Amanda could make a dash for the stairs. Without pausing to consider, she sprinted towards the basement with Amanda panting behind her. Jigging up and down with impatience, she waited for Amanda to

---

frantic – wild, ungestüm;
to sneak – *(hier)* schleichen

reach the bottom, then smeared the steps with sweet-smelling apricot **gloop**.

"Cool," said Amanda, who had finally realized what Isy was doing with Mrs Knosalla's shampoo.

"If he tries to come after us, he'll **skid** down the stairs," grinned Isy.

They raced towards the fitness centre to enlist the help of Dr Schley. The swimming pool was empty. They stared at the smooth surface of the clear blue water, hoping to see a tiny wave or ripple, anything that would betray the presence of an experienced swimmer who was holding her breath. But the dentist wasn't there.

"Dr Schley?" called Isy, running to the toilets. "Dr Schley?"

The drip-drip of a solitary shower communicated the unmistakable message: too late!

"Blast," muttered Amanda, checking the changing rooms. "She's gone."

Isy's heart sank. There was nothing for it but to search the upstairs bedrooms. Unless of course they tried to get back to the dining room and meet up with the boys …

She abandoned the empty tube of shampoo on the glistening tiles.

"As soon as we're upstairs, we need to shout at the top of our voices," she told Amanda. "The boys will hear us and come running." At least the brass band had stopped making such a **racket**. It was so

---

gloop *(slang)* – Glibber, schmieriger Stoff;
to skid – ausrutschen; racket – Krach

quiet you could hear a pin drop in the house. The only sound they were likely to hear was the **stealthy** tread of Mr Pumpkinhead.

At that moment, there was a terrific crash, then a series of thuds that sounded like a giant sack of potatoes tumbling down the stairs.

Later, when they were trying to put their emotions into words, they struggled to describe how they had felt at that moment. Time seemed to stand still, then they were swamped by an overwhelming **tidal wave** of fear. They ran for their lives.

"We can't hide there!" shouted Isy as Amanda headed for the changing rooms. "It's the first place he'll look."

They ran in the direction of the gym, and Isy **wrenched** open the heavy wooden door to the sauna. Fortunately the heater wasn't on. There was a good chance that Rainer Wutzke wouldn't notice the unlit wooden cabin. In a few minutes the first guests and villagers would return from the procession, and Isy hoped that someone would hear their cries for help and come to their rescue.

Summoning the last of their strength, they shut the heavy door behind them. The wooden walls were lined with benches of varying heights, but Isy and Amanda crouched uncomfortably on the floor, hoping that their pursuer wouldn't spot them through the window. Long moments passed as they

---

stealthy – verstohlen;
tidal wave – Flutwelle; to wrench – zerren;
to summon – *(hier)* zusammenraffen

waited in fearful silence. Rainer Wutzke's slow dragging steps were getting louder. As Isy had **predicted**, he searched the pool and the changing rooms first. His footsteps became heavier and more **ponderous**; he was obviously injured from his fall. Isy wanted to tell her friend that her tactic had worked, but she didn't dare talk, not even in a whisper.

At last the shuffling footsteps faded as he disappeared up the stairs. Isy could breathe easy again.

"We did it!" she hissed into the darkness. "He's gone!'

"I hate Cluedo, and I never want to see this house again!" stuttered Amanda between sobs.

"We haven't got out yet," said Isy soberly. She **clambered** to her feet and picked up their bags. The day had turned out to be more **fraught with** danger than she had imagined. Their adventures made detective shows like 'Polizeiruf' seem utterly harmless. She couldn't wait to go home.

Isy gave the door a **feeble** shove. She didn't panic when it didn't open: sauna doors had a tendency to **jam**. She tried again, then hurled herself against the stubborn wood. It was no use: the door wouldn't budge.

"Let me try," said Amanda, taking off her rucksack and throwing her weight against the door. She

---

to predict – vorhersagen;
ponderous – schwerfällig; to clamber – mühsam klettern;
to be fraught with – voll von; feeble – schwach;
to jam – verklemmen

rattled the handle and kicked the wood. It showed no sign of moving. Amanda's temper was beginning to **fray**.

"I can't believe it," she said crossly. "It's bad enough having to crouch on the floor in the darkness, and now we're trapped inside. It's a shame we can't have a sauna while we're waiting."

"Be careful what you wish for," warned Isy, pointing dismally to the temperature **gauge** which had just turned red. The air became pleasantly warm.

"You're not suggesting that he ...?" Amanda's voice trembled with horror. "He locked us in here on purpose, the pig!"

– 37 –

The two friends had stuck together through thick and thin.

They had hidden under a sofa from an intruder; they had been gagged and bound in a wild animal enclosure at the zoo; and they had escaped from a pair of kidnappers by clambering out of the attic of an abandoned house and fleeing over the rooftops.

But they had never been locked in a sauna and heated to a hundred degrees.

"I don't understand how he did it," wailed Amanda. "I didn't hear a thing, did you?"

---

to fray – ausfransen;
gauge – Messuhr

"Maybe he shoved a **broomstick** under the **latch**."

"Trapped by a broomstick!" groaned Amanda. She took a round object out of her jacket pocket and placed it near the glowing stones.

In the faint light of the oven, Isy could make out a small ball of meat. It was incredible; nothing could put Amanda off her food.

"It's all my fault," said Isy **ruefully** while the meatball sizzled succulently in the heat. "Remember how we'd been playing Cluedo at my place and I followed you through the rain? If I hadn't been so nosey, we wouldn't be in this mess!"

"No, but I'd probably be in prison by now."

"You could have explained the circumstances, and the judge might have let you off." She wiped the sweat from her forehead and took off her T-shirt. It was swelteringly hot. At first they had only removed their jackets and scarves, but as the temperature in the sauna continued to rise, they had discarded their jumpers, jeans and shoes. "How long do you think we can survive in here?" she asked in alarm.

She could picture the two of them in nothing but their underwear, dying of heat.

"What about Josepha?" shrieked Amanda, suddenly panicking. "What about our press conference? And our meeting with the chief of police? What about the reward?!" She took a deep breath.

---

broomstick – Besenstiel;
latch – Riegel; rueful – trübselig

"What if no one hears us? I bet my make-up is melting in my bag. Thank goodness the meatball is nice and warm." She took a big bite. "Do you want some?"

"No thanks," said Isy, torn between admiration and disapproval. "If only we had your mobile! I should never have told you to leave it in the kitchen. How could I have been so dumb?"

"It's lucky I ignored you."

"What? Brilliant, Mandi!" squealed Isy, bouncing up and down in excitement. "The boys will rescue us in no time! Thank God you've got your phone."

"Do you think it will work down here?" asked Amanda with her mouth full of meatball.

"Of course it will! They could bury you with a mobile, and you'd still have enough reception to make calls from the grave! Quick, phone Tannhäuser! Tell him to let us out!"

While Amanda rummaged in the dark for her mobile, Isy started to get dressed. "Don't burn yourself on the plastic," she said as Amanda held the pink phone to her ear.

"It's not too bad."

"What about your eggs? They must be thoroughly cooked by now."

"What eggs?"

"You told me to be careful with your rucksack. I thought you'd bought some eggs."

"Er, no, it's because..." Amanda waved her hand excitedly. Reginald had answered the phone.

"Can you hear me?" she bellowed. "We're in the

sauna! He locked us up! It's a hundred degrees in here! Yes, that's right, he's in the mansion, disguised as a pumpkinhead! Stop asking questions and get us out of here. We'll **evaporate** if you don't come soon!"

Despite the seriousness of the situation, Isy couldn't help giggling. "What did he say?"

"Not much. He had his mouth full of lettuce," said Amanda scornfully. "Ugh! How could anyone eat nothing but salad all day!"

She looked up sharply. "Did you hear that?"

"Hear what?"

"Footsteps!"

"What kind of footsteps?"

"I don't know! Just footsteps!" Amanda peered nervously through the window. "It can't be the boys, can it?"

"Not unless they've learnt to fly. Are you sure you heard footsteps?"

"There they are again!"

Amanda was right. Isy could hear them now as well. Someone was walking around outside. Amanda clutched her arm anxiously. Her fingers felt cold in spite of the heat. "He's coming back!'

"Don't be ridiculous," whispered Isy.

But the evidence was impossible to ignore.

Rooted with fear, they listened as the approaching footsteps came to a halt outside. Someone pushed a heavy object away from the door. At that moment, a face appeared at the window. No one

---

to evaporate – verdunsten

knew quite what happened next, but Amanda picked up her rucksack, took out a lumpy green object and took aim at the man who had appeared at the door. He groaned and sunk to his knees.

"Don't worry, it's not as bad as it feels," said Mr Rimpau behind him. "Aeschylus's prickles are painful, but you'll be able to tweeze them out. I had a similar experience myself last autumn in Altgrünheide..."

"Oh God," gasped Amanda, staring in horror at her weapon. "I was only trying to ... I mean, I didn't intend to ... Oh ..."

"Poor Rose **gets nobbled** by a cactus," murmured the detective, picking himself up with a wry smile. "Even the prickliest flower can't compete with that. Are you both OK?"

"Much better, thanks! How did you get here?" asked Isy, astonished. "We were locked in the sauna by Rainer Wutzke, aka Lothar Loll, aka Wolfram B. Braun. You've got to arrest him!"

"Do you mean the pumpkinhead?" enquired the detective. "We've apprehended him already. He wouldn't stop when we asked him to identify himself. He was trying to make a getaway in a stolen taxi, but he didn't get far with his broken leg ..."

Aha! thought Isy, *so it was Wutzke in the taxi ...* She elbowed her friend excitedly and pointed at Mr Rimpau's head. The crime writer's favourite protagonist, Detective Unmuth, wore a brown hat to protect him from the wind and rain. It explained

---

to get nobbled *(slang)* – außer Gefecht gesetzt werden

why the hat had seemed strangely familiar; and it explained who had been driving the **omnipresent** Golf!

The man in question was **glowering** at them from under his bushy eyebrows. "Am I right in supposing that this Rainer Wutzke works for a house-clearance company?" he asked sternly. "And is it possible that you lured him out of Berlin with the express intention of bringing him to this rather splendid house?"

"That's right. We wanted him to follow us to Brinkenbuhl," said Isy proudly. "And it worked! Now it's my turn to ask questions. Why were you following us?"

Mr Rimpau gave an embarrassed cough. "Well, a couple of days ago I saw a poster at the police station when I was visiting Detective Rose on matters **pertaining to** my book. In any case, I recognized the suspects and I decided that the angels were in need of a **guardian angel** of their own."

"Now you tell me!" growled the detective, looking **peeved**.

"I couldn't mention it earlier. These young ladies are particular friends of mine!"

"Thank you!" chorused Isy and Amanda, leaning forward to kiss his **stubbly** cheeks – Isy on the right, Amanda on the left.

---

omnipresent – allgegenwärtig; to glower – finster blicken;
pertaining to – im Zusammenhang mit;
guardian angel – Schutzengel; peeved – verärgert;
stubbly – borstig

"I was almost onto them anyway," said Detective Rose. "Amanda aroused my suspicions by fainting at the merest mention of her name. Rimpau called me forty-five minutes ago. I wasn't in the least surprised."

"As I was saying," continued Mr Rimpau breezily, "I saw your picture and decided to keep an eye on you. It turned out to be quite a challenge. I wasn't expecting to drive all the way to the shadowy village of Brinkenbühl to be met by a procession of ghoulish **revellers** gathered outside a converted mill. At first I thought the mansion was empty, but then I saw a pumpkinhead loitering in the hall. He was behaving rather oddly, and it occurred to me that a taxi driver matching that description had followed your blue Hyundai all the way from Berlin. At that point, I asked myself how Detective Unmuth would have handled the situation if he were here."

Patrick Mortimer Rimpau paused for a moment and fumbled in his brown tweed jacket until he found his pipe.

"My intuition told me that Unmuth would never have searched the mansion on his own. Unmuth would have called for **back-up**." He **inclined** his head towards Detective Rose. "And so I left the mansion and returned to my car to call the police. Helicopters are your favourite mode of transport, aren't they, Rose?"

---

reveller – Leute, die ausgelassen feiern;
back-up – Verstärkung; to incline – neigen

The detective smiled unhappily, and Mr Rimpau resumed his tale. "Everything went to plan. The helicopters landed in the garden, and Detective Rose punched the ferocious pumpkinhead to prevent him from crawling away on his broken leg. In fact, he knocked him out cold. I've done some amateur boxing in my time, and I can honestly say that I've never seen such an impressive **right hook**. And there you have it. Sadly, circumstances prevented me from indulging in my customary afternoon tea and cake ..."

"Don't worry," Isy reassured him, "there's a delicious buffet in the dining room that will make up for everything." She held out a key to the surprised detective. "It's for the broom cupboard in the kitchen. Josepha Boskov's locked inside. We saved her from Rainer Wutzke who was holding her to ransom. He told her a pack of lies and hid her in an apartment with the intention of stealing Mrs Boskov's inheritance. Josepha trusted him at first – but she'll tell you about it, I'm sure."

Footsteps and voices echoed through the basement: Gummy Bear and Tannhäuser were on their way to rescue the girls. Upstairs, Mrs von Leinungen was calling Harissa's name.

Amanda ran her hands flirtatiously through her damp hair. "Isy and I are ready to speak to the media. You can call the reporters, Detective Rose."

THE END

---

right hook – rechter Haken

A Few Weeks Later

It was ages – four, five or maybe even six whole weeks – since they had last been to Georgio's for a portion of delectable Italian ice cream.

Georgio's was the Bornsteins' favourite restaurant, and Isy never failed to be impressed by Amanda's **unruffled** confidence. Without her friend, she would never have dared to enter such an elegant establishment. A sheen of sophistication covered the dark wooden floor, starched white tablecloths and cut-glass **decanters**, and the exotic aroma of fresh cappuccino filled the air.

Isy loved Georgio's, and this time she was able to focus her full attention on enjoying her strawberry ice cream.

Josepha was safely home with her parents, the media frenzy had faded, and the front pages were no longer plastered with pictures of the girls and their proud parents shaking hands with the chief of police. Reporters had finally stopped lurking outside the school at break time, and the atmosphere in the classroom had settled down. The rest of 7b regarded Isy and Amanda with the usual mixture

---

unruffled – gelassen; decanter – Karaffe

of pride and envy, and their parents had stopped gazing at them dreamily over the rims of their coffee cups. Life was back to normal again.

Deep down, Isy and Amanda were **relieved** to get back to their daily routine and spend some more time with their families. They took the opportunity to write to Professor Pioschleck and apologize for the embarrassment they had caused.

Occasionally their thoughts turned to the man who had been arrested three weeks ago.

"It said in the newspaper that he wishes he'd learnt to play Cluedo," said Amanda, nibbling on a chocolate straw.

"It was a good thing he didn't," commented Isy. "I hate to think what would have happened if he'd known about the tunnels."

According to the police psychologist, Rainer Wutzke had a calm, steady temperament that was occasionally **blighted** by an excess of criminal energy. The criminal side of his personality came to the fore in situations of stress. Isy and Amanda knew from firsthand experience how **volatile** he could be. The real puzzle was why a man with a perfectly decent job would hold someone to ransom.

"It's always about money," sighed Isy.

"Speaking of which, have you decided what to do with your **windfall**?" asked Amanda, who had invested some of her share of the money in clothes

---

to be relieved – erleichtert sein; to be blighted – entstellt sein; volatile – explosiv; windfall – unerwarteter Gewinn

from a designer catalogue and was waiting for her new outfits to arrive. The rest of the cash had gone straight to her savings account. She and Isy had claimed the lion's share of the two thousand euros, while Gummy Bear and Tannhäuser settled for a third of the reward.

"I'm not sure," said Isy **hesitantly**. "Maybe I should save it and buy a better computer. I've got a new scanner, thanks to you."

"Thanks to *you*, you mean," Amanda corrected her. "You worked for the money, too. Besides, you can't put a price on friendship."

"How true!" said a familiar voice behind them. Mr Rimpau had arrived. "Do you know what Democritus said two thousand years ago?" He stopped to shake hands with Georgio who had rushed to greet the author and take his coat and scarf. "*Life is not worth living for the man who has not even one good friend.*"

"He also said: *A life without festivity is a long road without an inn,*" added Signore Georgio. "I can provide the inn as well as the friends and festivity." Everyone laughed.

Georgio escorted Mr Rimpau to the table that his wife Signora Violetta had laid for Detective Rose's guests.

"There's something we should talk about before the others arrive," whispered Isy. "I think it would be a good idea to, er… Well, to clear the air between us."

---

hesitant – zögernd

"So do I," nodded Amanda.

"I just wanted to tell you that I hadn't been spying on you or anything. I saw a text on your mobile when Mrs von Leinungen called to book her holiday angels. That's how I found out about Ruky. I honestly wasn't meaning to **pry**. I think that friends should be honest with each other, that's all."

"It's not always easy," said Amanda.

"But that doesn't mean we shouldn't try!"

"Sure!" said Amanda, jumping up to say hello to the other guests, who were flocking through the door. They sat down at the celebratory table with Tannhäuser, Gummy Bear, Mrs von Leinungen, Josepha, Mr Rimpau and their generous host.

"Let's celebrate the happy ending!" said the detective warmly. "You deserved it!"

He gave a short, **dignified** speech in their honour, then raised a glass of red wine to various people around the table and tucked into Signora Violetta's delicious antipasti. Isy and Amanda had to stop him from polishing off the lot. Once they had munched their way through mushroom ravioli, Tuscany rabbit with herb polenta, and scrumptious *panna cotta*, Mr Rimpau lit his pipe, Detective Rose ordered a grappa, Mrs von Leinungen sipped her cappuccino, Gummy Bear yawned, and Josepha told everyone **for the umpteenth time** about her

---

to pry – neugierig sein;
dignified – würdig;
for the umpteenth time – zum zigsten Mal

terrifying **sojourn** in the cupboard. Meanwhile, Isy slipped out to the cloakroom and placed something in the pocket of a long green coat. She put on her parka.

"What's the matter?" asked Amanda, who had suddenly appeared beside her. "You're not leaving, are you?"

"I'm afraid so. It's my parents' wedding anniversary and I'm supposed to be helping them celebrate. Have fun though! I'll see you tomorrow!"

Without waiting for a reply, Isy charged out into the heavy November rain. The pavement was covered in shiny dark puddles and cars sped past, throwing up shimmering droplets of spray. It reminded her a similar evening several weeks ago, but she couldn't remember exactly when. She raced through the rain towards the bright lights of the cinema.

She couldn't help feeling a bit guilty about Amanda, but what else was she supposed to do? *It's my first proper* ***date****,* thought Isy, her heart beating wildly. *Is he here yet? I wonder if he's bought the tickets?*

She stepped into the lobby and spotted him at the counter: a tall fair-haired guy with bright blue eyes, a **devil-may-care** attitude, and a habit of getting nosebleeds. He was wearing black jeans and a grey hoody with "New York" written across the front. He looked cool.

---

sojourn – Aufenthalt; date – Rendezvous;
devil-may-care – sorglos, unbekümmert

Isy was tempted to run over to him, but she waited for him to bring the tickets to her instead.

"Hi! All sorted?"

She nodded. "I put the pills in Detective Rose's pocket. I expect he'll give them to the narcotics division, and they'll get rid of the stuff."

"I'd love to see his face when he finds them!" laughed Janho. He stroked her warm cheeks shyly. "Thanks, Isy."

There was a moment's silence, then he smiled and asked, "Popcorn for the lady?"

She shook her head. The thought of eating anything made her ill. In fact, she didn't want to think about anything at all. It would be enough to sit next to Janho in silence and enjoy the fact that Josepha Boskov was nowhere in sight. The name of the film escaped her.

"You're famous now," whispered Janho as the lights went down. "I've seen your picture in the papers three times already! You'll have to tell me exactly what happened in Brinkenbühl."

Isy nodded. She felt as if she had been waiting for this moment forever. For a moment she felt perfectly contented. Suddenly the rustling of chocolate wrappers and popcorn bags reminded her that Amanda wasn't there. *I wonder what she would say if she could see me now,* she thought guiltily. To think that they had sworn to be honest with each other! *But it's OK to keep secrets sometimes!*

She sniffed the air longingly, breathing in the mouth-watering smell of honey-buttered popcorn. She was cross with herself for turning down

Janho's offer of popcorn – watching a movie without it wouldn't be the same. Sighing, she leant back in her chair and watched the **trailers**. Just then, a bag of honey-buttered popcorn appeared from the row of seats behind her, and Amanda said triumphantly: "Popcorn, anyone?"

---

trailer – Vorschau

Ebenfalls auf Englisch bei Thienemann erschienen:

Sabine Both: *Move to Cloud Nine;*
Love in my Luggage
Brinx/Kömmerling: *A Paul to Kiss*
Christamaria Fiedler: *Spaghetti Crime; Risotto Crime*
Sissi Flegel: *Forbidden to Love;*
Cool Kisses on the Beach
Bianka Minte-König: *Mobile Phone Love;*
Schoolyard Flirt & Catwalk Dreams
Hortense Ullrich: *Never Kiss a Witch; Love is Blonde*
Zimmermann & Zimmermann: *Maths, Stress and a Lovesick Heart; School, Trouble & True Love; Summer, Sun & Holiday Love*

Fiedler, Christamaria:
Pumpkin Crime
Aus dem Deutschen von Sally-Ann Spencer
ISBN 978 3 522 18114 3

Reihengestaltung: Birgit Schössow
Einbandillustration: Birgit Schössow
Schrift: Stempel Garamond und Remedy
Satz: KCS GmbH, Buchholz/Hamburg
Reproduktion: Medienfabrik, Stuttgart
Druck und Bindung: Friedrich Pustet, Regensburg

5 4 3 2 1° 08 09 10 11

www.thienemann.de
www.frechemaedchen.de